MW01074580

ADVANCE PRAISE

"In the complex world of pastors and church leaders Howard's *Freedom to Choose* provides fresh hope that decision-making in a creative, compelling and unifying fashion can take place. The author creates a helpful model for engaging the most challenging "what to do" cases of pastoral theology and practice (those not directly or specifically addressed by Scripture) and skillfully navigates the intersection of biblical texts, diverse Christian groups and different cultural settings. The book is intensely practical in that it provides a way forward for pastors and church communities feeling gridlocked and stymied by the tensions of applying Scripture where our questions seem misaligned or unanswered. A joy to read—delightfully accessible!"

William J. Webb,
adjunct professor of biblical studies at Tyndale Seminary in Toronto, Canada, and author of *Slaves, Women and Homosexuals, Corporal Punishment in the Bible*, and co-author of *Bloody, Brutal, and Barbaric?*

"This book fills a hole in the literature of biblical interpretation and applied ethics. Using his skills as a biblical scholar, professor, and pastor, Jim Howard takes us deep into Scripture in order to develop a model of addressing issues that Scripture itself does not directly address. His pastoral examples, taken from local church ministry and from cross-cultural settings, illuminate his ideas and their practicality. I commend this well-researched and wise work to anyone interested in how followers of Christ should live in light of the Bible's teachings."

Douglas Groothuis,
professor of philosophy at Denver Seminary and author of
Walking through Twilight: A Wife's Illness—
A Philosopher's Lament, Philosophy in Seven Sentences, and
Christian Apologetics: A Comprehensive Case for Biblical Faith.

"Blending a commanding knowledge of biblical studies, modern hermeneutics, ethics, and cross-cultural missions, and a rare gift for synthesis and lucid expression, Dr. James M. Howard examines when the Bible is at times seemingly paradoxical on how to live and what to do vis-à-vis the ethical spectrum of living the Christian life in the 21st century. I highly recommend this book."

Gene R. Marlatt,
vice president of academic affairs and professor of history at
American Pathways University, and author of
Logic and Critical Thinking, Ethics for the Third Millennium,
and *Journeys in Space, Time, and Beyond.*

"It wasn't until I had the pure joy of sitting under Dr. Howard's tutelage that I realized I'd been effectively holding my breath for decades in a subconscious attempt to justify my deep affection for rebels and ragamuffins while still maintaining the rubric of biblical orthodoxy. It has been such a delightfully liberating experience to discover that sound hermeneutics is not simply about grammar and syntax but must be understood within the metanarrative of redemptive history and the milieu of human experience. The material in this book dramatically impacted my personal life and ministry because it freed me from attempting to manipulate others to 'behave' and helped me anchor every single message I teach, write and live to the miraculously accessible, radically transformative, truly unconditional love of God!"

Lisa Harper,
author and international Bible teacher.

"With *Freedom to Choose*, Dr. James M. Howard fills a lacuna in the contemporary reflections about church matters in a pluralistic, relativistic, and rapidly changing society. Pastors, church leaders, and educators will find this unique approach to life issues both relevant and insightful for appropriate problem-solving in the church from a biblical worldview. It is a breathtaking resource for contemporary church leadership in a rapidly changing world we live in today."

Isaias Uaene,
Pastor and President of the Centro para o Desenvolvimento de Liderança (CDL) in Maputo, Mozambique, Africa.

"Those of us who take biblical authority with utmost seriousness regularly find ourselves bedeviled by the situations and decisions that confront us in our incalculably broken and convoluted world. How does biblical authority actually function in such scenarios to help us make faithful decisions when perfect or clean options are not even available? From his dual vantage points as a pastor and a New Testament scholar, Jim Howard gives us a model for bridging that gap both theologically and practically. I know this not merely from his manuscript but from watching him hammer out this model for years in the context of his ministry. He serves us well here—theologically, hermeneutically, and pastorally—by getting us out of our theoretical cul-de-sacs and echo chambers, raising the right kind of questions that will move us further down the paths toward embodied faithfulness."

Don J. Payne,
associate professor of theology and Christian formation at Denver Seminary, and author of *Already Sanctified*.

"*Freedom to Choose* is an important book—not only helpful, informative, interesting, and thoughtful—but important. In these pages Jim Howard is calling the people of God to learn and practice a discipline every parent and educator hopes their children and students grasp: critical thinking. Could it be that the Eternal Father and Master Teacher also intended for us to learn to humbly participate with the Word and the Spirit in the holy practice of critical thinking? And if so, how do we go about this process? Howard gives us practical and proven steps that equip us to joyfully and carefully work through unclear Bible passages and difficult life situations in a way that is fresh, life-giving, and faithful to our Lord and His Word. I believe this is important!"

Joyce Schroeder,
international Bible teacher and missionary
with Cadence International.

"The topic is timely, especially as church leaders rethink their ministry strategy in light of a renewed commitment to being missional communities concerned with outreach rather than simply attracting people to their place of worship. Pastors want help in sorting through the process of interpretation and application as they challenge their members to be people who think and act in terms of outreach and influence in their own neighborhoods and communities. I think there will be keen interest in this book."

David K Lowery,
senior professor of New Testament studies at
Dallas Theological Seminary.

"I need your book! Our families need your book. The issues you are addressing are front and center for both our family and our church. The pain isn't just 'out there' anymore."

Steve Garcia,
senior pastor, Celebration Community Church

Every church leader knows the challenge of applying the Bible to modern-day issues. Many ethical and practical questions with which people in the 21st century wrestle are not directly addressed in Scripture. That is why you need to read this book. It will not give you cookie-cutter answers. Instead, Howard's pastoral, redemptive, and field-tested approach will walk you through a process for engaging with contemporary issues that is thoughtful, faithful, and thoroughly biblical.

Gordon K. Oeste,
Teaching Pastor, Cedar Creek Community Church,
Cambridge, Ontario. Adjunct professor,
Tyndale University, and co-author of
Bloody, Brutal, and Barbaric?

So much of evangelicalism has focused on what is not allowed in the Christian life. This volume is a breath of fresh air as it encourages Christians to ask, what freedom do we have in Christ? Remaining grounded in the redemptive mission of scripture, Dr Howard presents a practical and accessible guide for church leaders and congregants to reflect theologically on the great possibilities afforded the church while remaining faithful to the character of God.

Lance Swearengin,
Senior Pastor, Conifer Community Church

FREEDOM
TO
CHOOSE

FREEDOM

TO

CHOOSE

What to Do When the Bible is Unclear

JAMES M. HOWARD

XULON PRESS ELITE

Xulon Press Elite
2301 Lucien Way #415
Maitland, FL 32751
407.339.4217
www.xulonpress.com

© 2020 by James M. Howard

All rights reserved solely by the author. The author guarantees all
contents are original and do not infringe upon the legal rights of any
other person or work. No part of this book may be reproduced in any
form without the permission of the author. The views expressed in this
book are not necessarily those of the publisher.

Unless otherwise indicated, Scripture quotations taken from the
Holy Bible, New International Version (NIV). Copyright © 1973, 1978,
1984, 2011 by Biblica, Inc.™. Used by permission. All rights reserved.
Printed in the United States of America.

Paperback ISBN-13: 978-1-6628-0525-7

Ebook ISBN-13: 978-1-6628-0526-4

DEDICATION

To those domestic and international students of mine, and
Christians everywhere who are working faithfully every day to
bring the wonderful story of the Bible into contemporary settings!

TABLE OF CONTENTS

PREFACE

This book began, as all books should, as a conversation and a
dream born out of practical questions. In 2013 I left the full-time
world of Christian higher education at Denver Seminary, much to the
surprise of some of my colleagues, to become senior pastor of Dillon
Community Church. Almost immediately I was faced with questions,
dilemmas, challenges, dreams, and theological disagreements for which
the Bible provided no clear direction.

Dillon Community Church (DCC) is a non-denominational
church situated in the high mountains of Colorado. With six world-
class ski resorts within 30 minutes, it is now largely a resort community. But it has not always been that way. In 1912, the Dillon Ladies
Aid Society started DCC in order to bring a Christian witness to the
valley. At this time, this area was largely mining and ranching, so you
can imagine the raucous nature that often described the local towns.
Starting a school, church, and law were the answers of the time to bring
and maintain order.

Since that time, with the growth of the ski industry, the county has
grown to become one of the premier skiing centers in the world. And
with the success has come people from all walks of life *and* a variety
of denominations from around the USA. With 3,000–5,000 annual
visitors to DCC, you can choose any area of discussion and you are
guaranteed to find varying and often opposing opinions! Depending
on the year, we have 3–5 different theological traditions among our
elders alone.

You may think this would be an impossible challenge. Quite the contrary! It has been one of the richest experiences of my life and a virtual on-going and live laboratory of how to use Scripture to navigate the many and diverse opinions of the church in contemporary times. Also, because of the highly transitory nature of the congregation, every sin you can imagine is present throughout the year! I then began to more fully understand the challenges of my young pastoral students in the Doctor of Ministry program, many of whom are located in churches scattered around the USA. To those former students and Christians everywhere who desire to bring an ancient text into the present world I dedicate this book.

But back to the present challenges. To assist me in working through these challenges, I invited my good friend Dr Don Payne to join me in the task of developing a better working model of theological integration and method. My own specialty is in biblical studies, specifically New Testament. His specialty is in theology and spiritual formation. Several years earlier we had begun lengthy discussions around theological method and how to bring our two specialties together in a fruitful way. I now had a real-life setting outside of the classroom to begin addressing the complex challenges that a variety of theological traditions bring to the discussion.

These discussions were very profitable and helped me to work through leading a theologically diverse church in such a way that not only allowed for unity, but actually *generated* unity along the way. Concurrent with my role as senior pastor, I was also teaching annually at schools and leadership conferences in Kathmandu, Nepal and Maputo, Mozambique. I began to bring many of our principles and ideas into those international contexts and soon learned better ways to both understand and apply the principles. Along the way, Don and I developed a Doctor of Ministry course for our beginning and new doctoral students, most of whom are pastors, leaders, or counselors, but all of whom have the same questions we had. I now apologize to those early students, both domestic and international, as they had to put up with a higher degree of disjointed ideas as they were developing. But to them, I owe a debt of gratitude for their enthusiasm, criticism, and general good nature as they wrestled with the principles in this book and worked to change their own approaches to theological method.

At the heart of this book is the question, "How do you bring the wisdom of the Bible to address a specific problem when the Bible does not give a singular or clear directive, or where the situation is radically different from that in the Bible?" The stock in trade of this book is that it brings the best in biblical studies and theological method together in order to make better and more faithful decisions that honor our Christian tradition(s).

No book is possible without the help of many. I am grateful for Tyndale House, Cambridge, England where I enjoyed a sabbatical in 2019. Kate Arhel, the deputy librarian, was indispensable for getting me all of the resources that I needed. It was at Tyndale House that I wrote the early draft chapters.

Additionally, there were several along the way who devoted significant time reading and interacting with my early draft. Thank you Don Payne, Gordon Oeste, Mike Maedo, Joyce Schroeder, Nancy Howard, and Karl Pagenkemper for your diligent early work. It is a much better work because of your comments.

Thank you to the members and elders of DCC who not only provided me with a sabbatical and time to write, but also endured many discussions about the principles outlined in this book. Similarly, thank you to the international students and leaders who provided indispensable feedback from their own cultural perspectives.

My wife, Nancy, was very patient to allow me to focus on this project. She has always believed in me and knew that what I was working on was important. She, more than anyone, is always aware of the internal stresses I bear from leadership and the anxiety I sometimes feel for people who struggle to agree and craft a way through the disagreements. Having lost my first wife, I cannot imagine life with her. Thank you and I love you.

But, most of all I am grateful to the Lord who made my education and experience possible. I love him dearly.

Enjoy! To God be the glory!

INTRODUCTION

Pastors and Christian leaders have a very real challenge on their hands today. How do they bring the wisdom of the Bible to address a specific problem when the Bible does not give a singular or clear directive, or where the situation is radically different from that in the Bible? What about where conflicting values are involved or when decisions are time-sensitive and must be made without all the facts? In these situations, how does biblical authority function and what does faithfulness look like on our part? This raises the real question of whether God intends that the Bible answer these questions directly, or does he desire something else from his people?

The Bible is rarely clear when dealing with the challenges of the 21st century. For example, a homosexual comes into your church environment where the church is divided on the issue of sexual orientation. How do you respond as a leader? Perhaps a teenager is confused about their best friend changing gender and requests to meet with you because they want to know how to interact with them in their new state. What advice do you give? When a younger member of your church understands that the Bible teaches against "friends with benefits," but does not agree with the Bible, do you simply open the Bible to point out "sin?" A resident of your community comes into your food bank smelling strongly of marijuana use, and yet has no money to buy food. Do you help them? Perhaps your church wants to put up an outside nativity display at Christmas, but the local residents are opposed. Do you exert your "rights" and keep moving forward?

In each of these cases, hermeneutics[1] and Bible study helps us to understand the Bible in its original context, but rarely helps us to directly answer the more modern questions arising in most churches (around the world) of how to think and what to do. Hermeneutics helps us think through the "gap" between us and the original context of the Bible, but we often find that the connection between our context and the context of the first century can quickly break down. Direct application is often harder to do than first imagined. The text answers questions, but often not the ones we are facing and have to answer today.

In 30 years of ministry in pastoral, leadership, and academic settings, at home and cross-culturally in several countries, I have consistently faced questions such as these. And they are typically not driven by age, gender, or religious background, but rather by a desire to apply the wisdom of God's Word in the contemporary world, or a personal circumstance that stands in opposition to their background and teaching.

When the Bible is not clear, I propose that an additional question needs to be asked; namely, what freedoms are granted by Scripture to develop redemptive approaches and manage the myriad of possibilities in any cultural setting? My purpose is to propose a methodology to answer that very question. My approach consists of a decision-making process followed by six principles to better work out application in modern settings. These principles serve as a "framework of interpretation"[2] by integrating key aspects of biblical hermeneutics, theological interpretation, and cultural analysis. I understand that this is a monumental task, but as a Christian who genuinely desires to learn from Scripture, these are the questions that I face on a regular basis.

A Word about Hermeneutics

So, do we actually need another book on interpretation and application? Before we answer that, it will be helpful to briefly survey the field of hermeneutics. Bernard Ramm, in his classic work, defined hermeneutics as "the science and art of biblical interpretation."[3] While there is no chapter on application, he does discuss the devotional and practical use of the Bible. He notes that the "Bible is more a book of principles than a catalogue of specific directions." He does note, in a one-paragraph section, that "commands in terms of one culture must be translated into our culture."[4] Apart from this, very little is devoted to the task of bringing the text forward into our culture today.[5]

Fortunately, the field of hermeneutics has moved a long way since the early works on hermeneutics.[6] The works addressing traditional hermeneutics have regularly been updated to include the latest in several technical areas; biblical studies, linguistics, archaeology, patristic studies, and other important areas. Do you have to master these other areas to do effective Bible study and bring the text into today's world? No! But you can have confidence that these areas are now considered in most commentaries and Bible studies. Additionally, along the way several additional key developments have occurred that better help us bring the Bible forward in more effective ways.

But first, in 1993, David Wells argued that evangelicalism had lost its way. Specifically, he argued that two models of pastoral ministry had dominated evangelicalism in the twentieth century. One model focused on theology as *doctrinal truth* in that theology had largely become irrelevant. The other model focused on *professionalism* wherein the practical needs that arose from pastoral demands had largely replaced good theology.[7] In my experience, Wells' observations still hold true at many levels today. Good theological method requires that we avoid the tendency to let pragmatism drive both our theological method and our decision-making. Rather, we should continue to work hard to blend the pragmatic needs of our people with the time-tested principles of both theological method and biblical study.

Regarding good theological method, John Stackhouse reminds us that, "When evangelicals have discussed methodology, we have generally preoccupied ourselves with the question of the nature and interpretation of the Bible. Clearly, however, evangelical theology is more than exegesis, so we need to attend to other dimensions of the theological task as well."[8] This book is a study on theological method which will become clear as the model unfolds.[9] But it is also intended to make this complex area of hermeneutics accessible to those who are faced with the day-to-day challenges of living as Christians in a fluid and agile culture.

As hermeneutics has evolved, missiologists have brought contextualization into the discussion. In 1979, Charles Kraft argued that one of the major areas of frustration for him and other missionaries was that much of the theology taught in both the academic world and the church world was insufficient to use in cross-cultural contexts.[10] I suspect that if you are reading this study, you have felt similarly. I know I have.

Dean Flemming has further argued that his cross-cultural missionary experience led him to rethink his approach to theology since many of the questions he was being asked were more culturally oriented. And yet he recognized that the answers to their questions needed both "biblical and theological answers."[11] In my experience, while the questions of the younger generation in America might be different than those of my students in other countries, they share a common desire to understand the Bible and theology in a way that make sense to them and to connect the Bible with their world in authentic and relevant ways.[12] The challenge we are facing today is engaging cultural challenges while simultaneously anchoring our decisions in good biblical theology.

Fortunately, the works addressing theological interpretation and Bible study have greatly aided us in our endeavor. God provides Scripture to the church for its transformation into the image of Christ, by the power of the Spirit, and to bring about redemption in the broader world. Since God created humanity with such diversity and beauty, we should not be looking for "cookie-cutter" Christian applications of the Bible. As any experienced missionary or pastor will tell you, part of the challenge they face is identifying the defining characteristics of a Christian in any culture, while simultaneously identifying areas of freedom. We will work to address this challenge in a simplified way.

And yet, while these works provide us with tools and theology that shape our approach to Scripture and our thinking as Christians, they generally do not provide an *easily accessible* methodology that answers the questions asked at the beginning.[13] This is partly due to the complexity and ever changing nature of the various cultural contexts and the problems they bring to the table. In my experience most Christians involved in church and Bible study have adequate familiarity with the Bible to handle the basic observations and interpretations of Bible study. Where they struggle is addressing the more complex challenges *in their current setting* where the Bible is unclear, and even understanding why obedience is important.

The church in the 21st century must be more agile than ever in recognizing and addressing these challenges. There is no indication that these challenges will cease or even slow down. With this in mind, I propose we think differently to address this need in our ever-changing world.

A Decision-making Model[14]

In a typical evangelical church leadership environment, the questions posed earlier often lead immediately to the question, "What does the Bible say?" Failure to clarify the problem at the beginning risks attempting to answer the wrong questions. Therefore, the first and most essential task is to develop a clear identification of the actual problem.[15] Once the problem is clarified, if the Bible does not directly address the problem or is unclear, an effective theological approach is to step back and ask a more basic question; namely, "What is our faithful response to be?" rather than, "What is the biblical thing to do?"[16]

In other words, is it possible to be "biblical" without being faithful to the redemptive nature and movement of God recorded in Scripture? Conversely, is it possible to be faithful, while deviating from a biblical imperative? I think both are possible. To answer these questions effectively, it is critical that the actual problem be clarified and stated in a way that allows both Holy Spirit guided experience and the Bible to play their proper and respective roles. The following decision-making scheme allows this:

1. Clarify the problem – a clear description of the problem or situation needs to be addressed. This could include complex situations in which there is no clear sense of biblical or theological guidance on how to respond, or situations that challenge your biblical or theological assumptions. Your ability to solve a problem is only as good as your understanding and definition of the problem.

2. Identify the informed collective intuition – an understanding of the collective intuition of the group involved in the decision-making process needs to be identified. Because we believe that the Holy Spirit guides the church, it is important to hear from the church.[17] Experience plays as significant a role as biblical training and understanding in addressing a complex problem. "What is your natural (Holy Spirit guided) instinct on how to move toward a solution?" This is demonstrated in James' letter representing the Jerusalem council, "It seemed good to the Holy Spirit and to us not to burden you..." (Acts 15:28 NIV).[18]

3. Identify and evaluate the related biblical and theological principles – once intuition has been surfaced and unified desires are emerging, it is appropriate to ask "What freedom does the Bible give us to live out our Christian principles and theology in this particular context, while still maintaining integrity with Scripture?"[19] Asking the question at this stage opens the discussion to a wider range of biblical and theological options than if we start with this step. Also, asking the question at this stage sets the framework that safeguards the integrity of our various theological traditions and orthodox faith statements.

4. Determine your range of options – what is the range of options available to address the problem or situation that is faithful to

both our Holy Spirit informed intuition and our review of applicable biblical passages and theological principles?

5. Decide the course of action based on the above process and evaluate for corrections or revisions as necessary.

Overview

The core of this study develops step #3 and works to identify and establish the freedoms granted by Scripture where the biblical texts are unclear or there are multiple, and perhaps even mutually exclusive, interpretations. This method consists of six principles to identify the freedom granted by the Bible. Following Miroslav Volf's proposal, these questions serve as a "framework of interpretation" by integrating key aspects of biblical hermeneutics, theological interpretation, and cultural analysis.[20] As we near the end of this process, these principles will also serve as a "test" to see if our decisions are faithful to Scripture. This book develops as follows.

Chapter 1 – Using Methods and Models. This chapter takes a more nuanced look into theological interpretation models and how they inform the decision-making process. In this chapter, I propose a model using the Bible itself on how to proceed as well as theological principles that will guide and shape our process of decision-making.

Chapter 2 – Expressing God's Love for a Broken World. This chapter addresses the first principle: our interpretation and decisions should lead to bringing God's love out to this broken world. This principle is related to the mission of God to bring redemption to his creation. If our practices, rituals, traditions, and behaviors as a church do not lead to this result, we should reexamine our interpretation. In this chapter, we are asking, "Does our use of Scripture and our resulting decisions lead to bringing God's love to a broken world?"

Chapter 3 – Engaging Culture with our Christian Ethics. This chapter addresses the second principle: our interpretation and decisions should lead to redemptive approaches in our current cultural setting. There is a difference between deciding to apply the Bible and the manner in which the Bible is applied. Just because the Bible specifies a behavior does not mean it must be followed in the precise way commanded. Church history is replete with examples of biblical directives that are either no longer applicable or have been lived out in ways different than their original setting. I will argue that guidance is necessary to make these sorts of decisions, if, for no other reason, than to help the surrounding culture understand why we do what we do. Our decisions must lead to redemption (or health) in our current cultural setting. In this chapter, we are asking, "Does our interpretation and resulting decisions lead to redemption in our current cultural setting?"

Chapter 4 – Keeping the Line in the Sand. This chapter addresses the third principle: our interpretation and decisions should be consistent with the freedoms established by the Bible itself. Following Stackhouse's lead, we see that the Bible often creates variation in its commands. For example, Paul encourages the young widows in 1 Corinthians 7 to remain single, but he advised the opposite in 1 Timothy 5, where they should remarry. Conversely, adultery remains inappropriate in all settings. This affirms the principle that where the Bible draws a line in the sand, so should the church. And where the Bible demonstrates variation, the church has freedom. This freedom does not mean freedom to do whatever we choose (Gal. 5), but is restrained by principles 1 and 2. In this chapter, we are asking, "Are our interpretation and decisions consistent with the freedoms established by the Bible?"

Chapter 5 – Following the Movement of God in Biblical History. This chapter addresses the fourth principle: our interpretation and decision should be consistent with the theological development of the Bible as it unfolds. This is asking a slightly different question than principle #3. As

N. T. Wright, William Webb, Christopher J. H. Wright and others have shown, the Bible demonstrates progression as it develops and unfolds. As such, applications and commands demonstrate movement and trends related to areas of social and personal concerns. This principle examines this movement and ensures that decisions regarding application are consistent with this movement instead of regressing. In this chapter, we are asking, "Are our interpretation and decisions consistent with the theological development of the Bible as it unfolds?"

Chapter 6 – Bringing the Kingdom into Our Present World. This chapter addresses the fifth principle: our interpretation and decisions should bring the eschatological kingdom into our present world. This is important so that the surrounding culture can more clearly see who God is and How his mission is being fulfilled in life-giving ways. This is the intent behind Christ's words that the will of God be done on earth as it is in heaven (the Lord's Prayer). Another way of saying this is that applications, rituals, and traditions done well bring Christ into clear focus now, while these same behaviors done poorly shield others from the truth and in some cases simply make them feel good. A note of caution here—the Bible also demonstrates that when a practice leads to offense within the surrounding culture, care should be given before moving ahead. In this chapter, we are asking, "Does our interpretation and resulting decisions bring the Kingdom of God into our present world?"

Chapter 7 – Creating a Flourishing Faith Community. This chapter addresses the sixth principle: our interpretation and decisions should lead to a flourishing community of faith. If our behaviors do not lead to a flourishing community, hypocrisy results and the mission of God is not fulfilled. A flourishing community is defined primarily as the consistent and proper integration of our stated theology together with our theology that is lived out every day. In every case where Scripture highlights discrepancies in this area, problems surface. It is crucial for churches to filter their practices through this lens to ensure their communities flourish. In this chapter, we are asking, "Does our interpretation and resulting decisions lead to a thriving and growing community of faith?"

Chapter 8 – Tying It All Together. This chapter summarizes the study and suggests implications for going forward.

My prayer is that you will agree with my argument, or at least part of it. Realistically, I expect that some will, and some will not. Whatever your reason for picking up and reading this book—scholarly, pastoral, or merely personal—I hope you will at least find something fresh to consider and something helpful as you interact with Scripture to make life-giving decisions in your own ministry. As Christians who take seriously the obligation and privilege of living out the Scriptures in our own settings, most of us have learned to depend deeply on the wisdom of the Holy Spirit, the guidance provided in the Scriptures, and the wonderful intuition and engagement of a healthy community of faith that is not daunted by the challenges brought to us from our cultures.

May this study bless you and give you more tools to better live out the gospel as you love your people—both those who believe and those who do not—those whom God has brought into your lives and churches.

Chapter 1

USING METHODS
AND MODELS

E arly on as a senior pastor, the elders approached me to take them through a notoriously complex theological issue and help them decide the best approach. Before starting that study, I asked them what were their criteria for choosing whether or not to obey New Testament directives? Their reply was "We obey the New Testament!" I asked them why their wives were wearing gold jewelry. They replied, "That was cultural!" Now, those trained in the interpretation and application of Scripture understand that this is an inappropriate use of the cultural criteria... all of the Bible is cultural. When pressed further, they realized that they had no identifiable criteria. They had simply always followed their pastor's lead. This surfaced in them a hunger and need to further develop a methodology for answering these types of questions.

In this chapter, I will take a more nuanced look into theological interpretation and how it drives the decision-making process. I will then propose from the Bible itself on how to proceed.

A Word about Application and Meaning

The general approach to application appropriately tries to understand and identify what God desires of Christians as they interact with the world around them and their Christian traditions. Scott Duvall and Daniel Hays state, "When you identify the theological truths or principles conveyed by a passage, you are discerning what is timeless in the passage and beginning to bridge the gap between the biblical text and the contemporary world."[21] Similarly, William Klein, Robert Hubbard, and Craig Blomberg argue that "every sentence, indeed every verse, appears as part of a larger, coherent unit of thought that has some relevance for us."[22] I agree and am deeply grateful for these scholars who have invested much time and energy into producing helpful and effective resources for the church.

The question that motivates me is more related to topics *not directly* addressed by the Bible. In these cases, I propose that we ask the further question, "What freedom does the Bible give us in culturally different or complex situations to live out our Christian principles?"[23] How we respond to this question largely depends on our culture and corresponding values. This requires analysis beyond the traditional approaches to hermeneutics.[24]

At this point, it is helpful to wrestle briefly with one of the great challenges of hermeneutics; that of determining meaning. This is a very complex area of study with voices from many camps vying to be heard, especially with the movement toward postmodern criticism and philosophy. I do not intend to engage in this debate except with a few caveats.[25]

First, I hold a high view of Scripture. I am not proposing a postmodern reading of the text. I hold to orthodox beliefs including absolute truth about what the Scriptures convey about God and his character, even though how we relate to each other in our faith communities and to the broader world around us is often highly relative. So, it is important to know that I am not proposing that "anything goes."

Second, I take the "plain reading" of Scripture to mean discovering what the original authors intended in their cultural setting. As anyone who is trained in hermeneutics and Bible study knows, it is hard work to even get a glimpse of this intent. And yet, to fail to wrestle with this task leaves open a very wide door for unintended meaning and even misunderstanding of meaning which often leads to inappropriate conclusions in our various settings today. Therefore, I believe it is our responsibility to work toward this goal. "The reader is a positive, not negative, force in interpreting a text. I have argued here that the original meaning of a text is not a hopeless goal but a possible and positive and necessary one. A text invites each reader into its narrative world but demands that the person enter it on its own terms."[26]

Third, I am not proposing a "literal" reading of Scripture. In my experience many Christians in conservative evangelical traditions use this term with little clarity as to its meaning and implications. The Bible is rich in figurative language, all of which is used to convey meaning in any given type of literature used by the authors within different cultural settings. The vast majority of evangelical hermeneutics texts give ample instruction and principles to demonstrate how to navigate this wonderful area of interpretation.

Finally, I firmly believe that all Scripture is redemptive in nature (2 Tim. 3:16–17). But this does not mean it directly applies or is directly redemptive in all of our situations today. The concept of redemption will be defined and clarified later in the book. This does mean that it is incumbent on us to develop the criteria by which we determine when to obey a passage the way it is written or to contextualize it in today's culture such that it is still redemptive as originally intended.

A final note. I have taught cross-culturally for many years and have noticed a pattern related to teaching the Bible. There is a difference between biblical principle and cultural practice. As an educator, I have become keenly aware of when I am crossing that line. When I am being asked "what do you mean?" questions relating to the principles and meaning of a text, I am teaching in the realm of biblical principle. When the questions progress to application "how do we do this?" I have moved into the realm of cultural practice. At this point, if I attempt to answer the application question I significantly increase the risk of being imperialistic and attempting to persuade them to become like me—an

American evangelical, trained in a conservative evangelical tradition, and belonging to the Boomer generation. This is not my purpose.

Similarly, I found the same to be true as a pastor. Several of the high school students in our church once wanted my counsel on how to live out their faith on the football team. I realized that if I answered that question, I had moved beyond biblical principle to cultural practice. Following the pattern I had established overseas, I transitioned to a facilitator role and began asking them questions about their cultural setting. As Millennials, it was somewhat different than mine. It did not take them long to begin to develop ways to live out their faith that were far better than what I would have proposed. This is an example of the freedom and responsibility that we have as pastors and educators. Our goal should be to help our people not only grasp the meaning of a text, but to create new and fresh ways to live it out with integrity to Scripture within their own context.

Effective theological method steps back and asks a more basic question; namely, "What is our faithful response to be?" rather than, "What is the biblical thing to do?" We may not always be able to be "biblical," but we should always be faithful. I realize this may come as a surprise to many of you. This will become clearer as the study progresses.

What then are the criteria we use to determine when to obey a passage the way it is written or to develop a more redemptive solution that fits our current cultural context? Another way of asking this is, "What criteria are needed to identify our freedom and guide us when we deviate from the text?" This is where a closer look at theological method and interpretation will aid us.

Theological Hermeneutics

The growing field of theological hermeneutics or theological interpretation has made promising advances to help pastors, leaders, and those engaged in Bible study get past the question of biblicism and move toward better theological method.[27] Miroslov Volf has proposed using a "framework of interpretation" to guide and safeguard any interpretation.[28] His proposal presents a helpful model that gives both a framework that delimits the interpretation to ensure it fits within the doctrinal statements of most churches as well as the deeper convictions that lead to obedience and Christlikeness. This is helpful as we do not want to deviate from our Trinitarian roots, for example.

At the same time, Joel Green argues that the emerging Rule of Faith in the early church was in effect statements about their beliefs.[29] The Rule of Faith was a confession of beliefs that represented those teachings of the Apostles that were considered authoritative.[30] They provided guidelines for both the worship practices in the early church and interpretation of Scripture, and even became a primary criterion for selecting which books made up the New Testament.

This is helpful for our present study because the Rule of Faith was developed prior to the establishment of the present New Testament canon. "From a historical perspective, we cannot argue that the church's Rule of Faith is built on top of the foundation provided by the Old and New Testaments."[31] The New Testament collection was being identified alongside and in relationship to these "kerygmatic formulations." Thus, the Rule of Faith and the canon of Scripture took shape in a "context of mutual influence."

Green goes on to point out that what separated the early church from the approaches of Jewish leadership was not related to Scriptural authority or knowledge of original languages. New Testament studies have long demonstrated that the Old Testament was read from a variety of perspectives at the time of Jesus. For example, the early Christians, in contrast to the Pharisees, read the Scriptures in a certain way that located the life and ministry of Jesus as the focal point of the Old Testament. They had different hermeneutical assumptions about how to understand and apply the Scriptures faithfully within their own communities. To ensure some degree of consistency, the early church developed "Christological lenses" by which to interpret Scripture. "These hermeneutical lenses came to be codified in the Rule of Faith."[32]

The Scripture and Hermeneutics Seminar goes one step further and argues that theological interpretation presupposes its own hermeneutic. In other words, our method of interpretation is fundamentally shaped by our understanding of the Christian story and that this story is the story in which every other story finds its place. Thus, a core requirement is that our method of interpretation must also make its case to the wider world. This invites us to see hermeneutics and theological interpretation as a delightful exercise that balances truth and love and is deeply pastoral. As an evangelical, I agree with Heath Thomas when he states, "God provides Scripture to the church for its transformation into the image of Christ, by the power of the Spirit."[33]

All of these approaches are moving the discussion toward better thinking, especially when it comes to culture and how we are to live within and bring truth into the light in our cultures. While there is "nothing new under the sun," there are certainly more unique and complex ways of sinning. Additionally, as culture shifts its foundational moral base,[34] the issues that define culture in any specific location are making their way into our churches in increasing numbers.

The final area for us to consider before we define our method relates to culture. Paul Hiebert helpfully defines culture as "the more or less integrated systems of ideas, feelings, and values and their associated patterns of behavior and products shared by a group of people."[35] The task before us is to understand how the gospel engages the cultural and social worlds in which we live.

As I have ministered in the evangelical tradition all my Christian life, it has become clear to me that our perspective of the gospel is both good and inadequate. We have been taught, appropriately, that the gospel is the good news about Jesus' death on the cross and subsequent resurrection (1 Cor. 15:1–8). But the gospel is so much more than that. For example, Jesus' descending from David is also part of the gospel (2 Tim. 2:8). The fuller picture of the good news of Christianity is that God has not forgotten his fallen creation. Not only will he renew the entire creation, but all of history is moving to accomplish God's desire to bless all of the nations. This is why Paul can powerfully declare, "Scripture foresaw that God would justify the Gentiles by faith, and announced the gospel in advance to Abraham: 'All nations will be blessed through you'" (Gal. 3:8).

For the purpose of our study, it is important to understand that culture needs to be viewed differently in different locations. Using Hiebert's definition above, the culture in Kathmandu, Nepal is quite different from that in my own church. Similarly, it is also true that the culture of Fairview, Oklahoma is different, in substantial ways, than my own church. This means that our method needs to interact with Scripture *and* culture such that contextualization—bringing all of the message of the Bible to bear—allows for differing cultures with differing values.[36]

The fact that the testimony of the biblical texts is not always clear in relationship to specific modern circumstances raises a potential risk. Should churches in every culture treat the problems in their churches the same way the world over? I think not. Even in my own country, the values espoused in the different regions throughout the country are quite diverse.[37] The same is true for the different cross-cultural settings in which I teach every year. There must be room for divergent opinions on how to discern wisdom from the Scriptures in handling these differing complex situations. This is what Lesslie Newbigin is getting at when he asks, "If we do not accept a total relativism in respect of the varieties of human culture, what degree of relativism can there be?[38]

A Proposed Set of Methodological Commitments[39]

As we work to specify the questions that will guide our use of Scripture, it is important to lay out the methodological commitments— the framework of interpretation—that will shape how the questions are formed and asked. From these commitments, we will then develop the specific questions that need to be answered as we make decisions.

Commitment to the grand story. To avoid various traps, pitfalls, and rabbit trails, our method needs to be based on strong, yet creative theology of Scripture. The Bible is a narrative that tells the grand story of God's redemptive acts in history, culminating and centering on the work of Christ. This means that we must carefully consider the historical, cultural, and literary dimensions of the Bible.

Commitment to redemption. The church is the primary context for theological interpretation as well as the primary means of living out the decisions made. Since God has called people for his own glory and mission, it is critical that our method be oriented toward creating a redemptive atmosphere where people can realize genuine hope in the midst of struggle. The story of Christ can then become our story. It is a story which the world needs to hear and see lived out.

Commitment to the mission of God. Since a central theme in the Bible is God blessing the nations (Gen. 12:3; Gal. 3:8), our method must capture the missional aspect of the Bible. This means that we need to always be attentive to the theme of mission and what God wants to accomplish through our churches as we make decisions that impact our various cultures.

Commitment to the transformation of the church. In the context of the mission of God, our method must also take into account the goal of decision-making: the transformation of the church into the image of Christ. As churches live out their faith in their own cultures, they are transformed and become more Christ-like. This becomes the primary catalyst to capture the world's attention. Therefore, it is imperative that our decision-making lead to healthier churches.

Commitment to the unity of the Bible. Since the Bible is a unity, our method must articulate the coherence of the Bible using the concepts derived from the Bible itself. In my experience, most Christians approach Scripture as a collection of moral instructions, stories, spiritual nuggets, and so forth without a coherent overarching framework. Our people need to understand *the unified story of redemption*.[40]

With these commitments in mind, let's look at the Scriptures themselves to see if there are helpful examples. The interpretive principles proposed, and questions asked by this study are all grounded in many years of wrestling through numerous passages to determine both how theology is revealed by God and how it operates in any cultural context.

A Way through the Maze

Some years ago, I began to notice a pattern in Scripture in which "adjustments" were made either to the law or to the way people lived out the law. These stories perhaps provide a way through the maze of decision-making using the Bible as the basis. The following are representative examples.

Numbers 27:1–11. In Numbers 27 the daughters of Zelophehad petitioned to have "their right to hold the land west of the Jordan."[41] According to Numbers 26:52–55, the land was to pass on to the male heirs. So, the daughters approached Moses and Eleazar and petitioned a change so that they would not be left without a family inheritance. It is important that it was the daughters who initiated the challenge since one of the key questions regarded the status of women in Israelite society, particularly the right to own land in the Promised Land. Moses brought the matter before the Lord wherein he agreed with the daughters. "There then follows a statement of law: As an exception to the rule that only a son qualifies as his father's direct heir, it was ordered that the ancestral territory of a man who died without leaving a son would pass to his daughter."[42] The noun used in Lev 27:7 to describe the daughters' petition is used elsewhere with a legal connotation in mind.[43] This means that the daughters were requesting a change in the code and God accommodated them. But not only did he accommodate them, he assured that future generations of women could legally receive property.[44] Why would God do this?

This passage reveals that the law does not speak to everything. From the story we see something of the character of how the law works, beyond simply the commandments themselves. In other words, the law, given in a cultural context, leaves us with the understanding that applying it beyond the written code requires wisdom. This in turn invites us to look for larger principles in how God sees application of the law to prevent undue, unneeded or unwarranted restrictions. In this case, it appears that God's willingness to revise the inheritance laws was related to gender relations. Male ownership was the common practice among the "patriarchal social and cultural milieu of the period among most Semitic peoples."[45] The challenge of the daughters and God's subsequent revising of the inheritance laws represents an *advancement* in cultural ethics regarding women's rights in the ancient world.

2 Chronicles 30. In 2 Chronicles 30 Hezekiah led the southern kingdom to celebrate the Passover together with citizens from the northern kingdom (2 Chron. 30:1, 25). For our purposes, what is unique about this passage is, first, Hezekiah led the people to celebrate it at a time which was not "regular" (2 Chron. 30:2).[46] Second, they were unable to celebrate the Passover at the regular time because there were not enough consecrated priests (2 Chron. 30:3). Third, when the time came to celebrate it, the people themselves were unclean and had not purified themselves, "contrary to what was written" (2 Chron. 30:18).

In Hezekiah's situation, prior to their eating the Passover, he prayed for them requesting the Lord to pardon them for eating the Passover differently than prescribed (2 Chron. 30:18–20). The Lord heard his prayer and healed the people. Hezekiah had assured the people that God was gracious and compassionate and would not turn his face from those who turned to him (2 Chron. 30:9). Here Hezekiah acted alone (in contrast to v. 2) and conceded that most of the people had violated the purification requirements. In faith he asked God for permission to deviate from the prescribed ritual and God granted his petition. What gave Hezekiah the confidence to lead the nation differently than the prescribed requirements concerning the Passover? A bit of cultural background will help answer this question.

The northern kingdom had been destroyed by the Assyrians, and Hezekiah was inviting the remnant to join Judah in celebrating the Passover (2 Chron. 30:6). The refugees coming from the north would have impacted the southern kingdom. This was a significant factor in

Hezekiah's decision. "Bethel had been refurbished as a center of religion (2 Kings 17:28) and syncretism was rampant (2 Kings 17:29–34) throughout the Assyrian province of Samaria. Now was the time to appeal to the true followers of Yahweh in Israel."[47]

This story reveals that the needs of the nation to humble themselves and return together to the Lord took precedent over the prescribed rituals involving Passover. Hezekiah understood God to be gracious and compassionate (2 Chron. 30:9). What was more important than the prescribed rituals were the return of the people to the Lord. Hezekiah could pray with confidence that the Lord would pardon everyone "even if they are not clean according to the rules of the sanctuary" (2 Chron. 30:19–20). Once again, we see something of the character of the law, and how higher priorities can supersede the prescribed rituals.

Acts 10–11. When we turn to the New Testament, we see a similar pattern. The story of Cornelius and Peter is well-known. However, there are some interesting details in the story that impact our study. As the gospel mission turned to the Gentiles, Peter (and the Jews) needed to "recalibrate" their view of the law and God's expectations. At issue in this text was both the content of the food as well as who could share the food. The basic point of the story is the acceptance of uncircumcised gentiles into the fellowship of God's people after they had become believers in Jesus.[48]

The dietary laws of Israel are a complex area of legal regulations (Lev. 11).[49] For our purposes, the following points are significant. First, Peter's refusal to kill and eat reflected his strong conviction to fulfill God's commands that Israel should never eat anything that was profane or unclean. For Peter, this would have included eating forbidden animals as well as eating with Gentiles, both of which he had considered impure and profane. Second, the rebuke from God that he should not consider impure what God had cleansed reflects the main point of the vision (Acts 10:15–16). God had now declared all animals to be clean. This implies the rituals relating to the dietary laws were no longer in effect. Peter was left with the simple choice of changing his theology and behavior, or not. The repetition and the removal of the sheet back to heaven strongly communicated the permanence of these changes since "the holy God would not take anything profane into the presence in heaven."[50]

What is now evident is that God had initiated a new order. The following sections (Acts 10:27–43; 11:1–29) revealed that this surprising turn of events was far outside the comfort zone of both Peter and the believers in Jerusalem. The implications are astounding. As Peter explained to Cornelius, it was against their laws to associate or even visit with a Gentile (Acts 10:28). The vision had revealed that the previous distinction between "them" and "us" was no longer valid. The dietary laws had to be rescinded in order for close fellowship to occur. This reflects a core motivation of God to reach the nations—the very promise to Abraham (Gen. 12). The result was great joy and praise (Acts 11:18). This sets the stage for the next great challenge in Acts 15.

Acts 15. As we turn to the Jerusalem Council we see the leaders now being asked to make decisions about the role of the law—specifically prompted by the issue of circumcision—regarding Gentiles who were coming into the church. The dispute originated from the ministry of Paul and Barnabas. To resolve the dispute, they all gathered in Jerusalem with the apostles and elders. Some of the Pharisees felt that the Gentiles had to be circumcised and required to keep the law of Moses (Acts 15:5). Peter, referring back to his experience with Cornelius, argued that it was God who made the choice to accept the Gentiles, the evidence of which was the giving of the Holy Spirit (Acts 15:7–11). This led the leaders to craft a letter asking the new Gentile believers to obey four of the legal commands (Acts 15:29). On what basis did the apostles reduce the requirements of the law to these four?

Two factors played a significant role in their decision-making. First, Peter's experience with Cornelius had demonstrated that a new order had been instituted by God. The second factor was the earlier example of how Jesus handled the law (Matt. 12:1–8). We will come back to this second factor.

In Peter's dialogue, he based his approach on what he had seen God do earlier with Cornelius. Based on that experience, Peter urged the leaders to be careful not to put a yoke on the Gentiles that their ancestors had been unable to bear (Acts 15:10). Peter emphasized that God had accepted them as Gentiles without circumcision and submission to the law. As part of Peter's defense, regarding the excessive burdening of the Gentiles, he warned the Jewish believers against testing God by resisting that which was so clearly of his doing. This means that they were in danger of unbelief and mistrust of God and even finding fault with God's actions! This potentially represented a direct challenge against God.

James picked up on this experience and similarly decided that the council's decision should not make it difficult for the Gentiles to turn to God (Acts 15:19). This reasoning appeared in the letter sent to the Gentiles (Acts 15:24, 28). In the letter, their reasoning was clear. It was based on their experience and the ministry of the Holy Spirit. "The council of apostles and elders focuses on establishing a *theological solution* (vv. 7b–19) before providing practical guidance for Gentile believers and their interaction with Jewish believers (vv. 20–21)."[51] It is intriguing that their prior experience in Acts 10 forced them to wrestle with a theological conclusion arising from a specific *experience*, which then led to specific *application*. How often do we encourage this process in our churches today?

What is surprising is that, of the many issues and sins for which the Gentiles were known, they singled out only four restrictions. These four restrictions were abstaining "from food sacrificed to idols, from blood, from the meat of strangled animals and from sexual immorality" (Acts 15:29). It is not that the other issues were unimportant, as Paul's letters attest, but that these four issues were important as the Gentiles began coming into the church and the Jews and Gentiles had to live side-by-side as the new people of God.

The rationale for these four stipulations is disputed.[52] Perhaps the best solution is found in the letter itself. The council was concerned about restoring unity and peace in the church (Acts 15:24) as well as creating a pathway into the church that Gentiles could easily follow (Acts 15:28). The fact that the Acts account recorded their concern to avoid "excessive burdening" three times is significant (Acts 15:10, 19, 28). Clearly, the apostles were responding to their experience and being careful to live out what God had already accomplished. While there were more stipulations related to resident aliens in the law, these four were chosen to facilitate the concerns expressed in the letter. This allowed the Jews and Gentiles alike to welcome each other in ways that were non-offensive to each group.

The bottom line is that the apostles and elders felt free, under the wisdom they had gained from the Holy Spirit ("it seemed good to the Holy Spirit and to us"), to make these adjustments without a direct word from the Lord. Rather, they were working out the implications of God's unusual actions in the life of Cornelius and their experiences on the first missionary journey of Paul and Barnabas. Acts 15:31 says the receiving churches (especially Antioch) rejoiced because of this encouraging development.

Matthew 12:1–8. The second factor that played a significant role in the council's decision-making was the example of how Jesus himself handled the law. A key example is captured in the story of Jesus going through the grain fields on the Sabbath.[53] The basic story is that the Pharisees challenged Jesus because his disciples were "doing what is unlawful on the Sabbath" by eating heads of grain (Matt. 12:1). The Pharisees' charge was in keeping with Moses' teaching which forbade work on the Sabbath, which could encompass gleaning (Exod. 31:13–14; 35:2).[54]

Jesus' response shifted the core issue away from labor on the Sabbath as the Pharisees charged. Rather, he introduced the more significant issue of eating food which was allowed only to priests. Jesus' response appealed to Scripture to demonstrate that God expected "the legal statements to be qualified in practice"[55] What is intriguing is that he appealed to the narrative tradition, rather than legal statements, to argue for the significance of human needs over the legal requirements. This is important as, unlike his opponents, "Jesus had based his ethics on Scripture, and Matthew contends that Jesus' ethics reflect a more biblically sensitive approach than those of his opponents."[56] Using the story of David, he argued that hunger, and more broadly human well-being, overrode the law. Jesus is not only challenging their interpretation of the Sabbath, but their entire method of interpreting the law.[57]

Jesus' response revealed a principle that is also found in the Jerusalem council discussions; namely, the law is subordinate to human needs in that *there is a higher principle at work*. In David's case it was hunger. David Rudolph has persuasively argued that Jesus accommodated himself to "another's customs or way of life" for the purpose of his mission. "All three synoptic gospels record that Jesus ate with 'tax collectors and sinners' (to the consternation of the Pharisees) in order to 'save' the lost (Luke 19:7–10) and 'call' disciples (Mark 2:14, 17; Matt. 9:9, 13; Luke 5:27, 32)."[58] Rudolph's concept of accommodation does not mean that Jesus violated the law but demonstrated freedom with the boundaries of observance. "Jesus' statement 'I have come to call not the righteous but sinners'... and his parable of the lost sheep (Luke 15:7), suggests that his ministry to sinners was not an ancillary aspect of his ministry; it was central. In fulfilling his mission, accommodation was essential."[59]

Jesus then went further and introduced the contradiction of the priests working in the temple on the Sabbath. "By the fact that the priests engage in temple duties on the Sabbath (preparing the consecrated bread, presenting offerings, cf. Num. 28:9–10), they too are guilty of Sabbath violations."[60] Even though allowed by the law, it still represented an exception to the legal code. Jesus took it further here with the use of a traditional Jewish "how-much-more" argument. The various rabbinic traditions made provision for certain conditions to override the law (i.e., the saving of a life). Jesus here ranked his own authority above the temple when he claimed that "something greater than the temple is here" (Matt. 12:6) and above the Sabbath when he claimed "the Son of Man is Lord of the Sabbath" (Matt. 12:8). In other words, if certain conditions allowed for deviating from the law, *how much more* the fact that Jesus as Lord of the Sabbath was an even greater condition? The implication is that if the priests who serve the temple on the Sabbath are innocent, how much more the disciples who serve the one greater than the temple on the Sabbath as well?

Jesus' final surprising statement was to quote Hosea 6:6 (Matt. 12:7). His assumption was that the Pharisees did not truly understand the mercy of God. In the Hosea passage, the use of *hesed* (mercy) revealed a great deal about Jesus' accusation here. The concept of *hesed* is a very rich concept in the Old Testament that is related both to God's character and his incredible love for his people. At its core, it has the idea of covenant faithfulness.[61] In the Hosea passage, while God was faithful to his covenant, his people were not. This is the basis for God declaring, "For I desire mercy, not sacrifice, and acknowledgment of God rather than burnt offerings" (Hosea 6:6). "They do not seem to know what loyalty means."[62] Indeed, as Hosea had identified many years before, their "love" (*hesed*) was fleeting, "Your love (*hesed*) is like the morning mist, like the early dew that disappears" (Hosea 6:4).

As it appears throughout the Old Testament, *hesed* clearly has more than simply covenant faithfulness in view. The basis of *hesed* is strongly relational and describes "the disposition and beneficent actions of God toward the faithful, Israel his people, and humanity in general."[63] It is God's love that is foundational to his faithfulness to his covenant. Thus, it is translated in a variety of ways in the Old Testament, including lovingkindness.

In the Matthew passage, Jesus exposed the hypocrisy of the Pharisees by his use of Hosea 6:6. He accused the Pharisees of neglecting the more important matter of God's deep love for people and choosing, instead, their commitment to their traditions. In effect, he accused them of neglecting *their responsibility as leaders to model this deep love and loyalty.* "Jesus is saying that mercy rather than legal observance is the heart of God's will and that he has correctly exemplified this with respect to his disciples, who are thereby 'guiltless' before God."[64]

Everything in the story moved toward his conclusion that "the Son of Man is Lord of the Sabbath." Not only does Jesus have absolute authority over the Sabbath, but with his actions he revealed that he is also the final interpreter of the law. He is greater than the temple and greater than Sabbath. Something greater has come - Jesus. It is no wonder that the disciples at the Jerusalem council could reshape their approach around not being a burden to the Gentiles. As Craig Keener has argued, this story provides a "hermeneutical key for many of Jesus' nonlegal teachings"[65] and, I would suggest, a model for how to appropriate Scripture when looking for God's wisdom amidst unclear and complex situations in life.

Summary

There are other passages that could be used, but these are sufficient to demonstrate that there were many situations not covered by the law and they allow us to summarize key principles when it comes to using the Bible, especially where the Bible may not reveal clear application. Each of these principles will be developed in the model presented in this study.

First, we must remember that God has initiated a new order. This takes the form of the New Covenant. Gentiles coming into the church provide an example of how the church should embrace and reach out to people who are different in their culture, ethnicity and even their sinful patterns. The distinction between the "them" and the "us" carries far less power than ever in the biblical narrative.

Second, experience plays a vital role in discerning the guidance of the Spirit. The decision-making journey will always involve the tension of maintaining unity and peace within the church, and fidelity to Scripture, while simultaneously creating pathways that welcome people stuck in their sin or marginalized because of their sin.

Third, each of these stories reveal some degree of human freedom when interpreting and applying Scripture. Does this mean they had freedom to do whatever they desired? Clearly, no. What freedoms we have and do not have will become clear as we build our method.

Fourth, the church should take seriously Peter's warning about not testing God. In looking at Christ's example concerning the Sabbath, it is clear that Jesus was challenging their entire method of interpreting the law *and applying it in their own cultural context.* When Jesus ranked himself above the temple, he provided a model of christologically interpreting how the Bible is to function within church life.

Finally, the most important priority is to express and maintain a love for sinners that matches God's own deep love and follows the examples of Christ's expressing that love for the sinners in his world. There truly is a higher principle at work, and we the church would do well to remember that the law is subordinate to human well-being.

With these principles in mind, we move on to develop the specific principles (and related questions) of how to determine what freedom we have when the Bible does not give a singular or clear directive or where the situation is radically different than that in the Bible.

Chapter 2

EXPRESSING GOD'S LOVE FOR A BROKEN WORLD

I t is very common in church environments for decisions to be made without any conscious thought given to the mission of God. For example, in a discussion with the facilities committee in our church, I asked them what they understood their purpose to be. They replied that their purpose was to upgrade and keep the facilities operating and manage all maintenance contracts. I asked them how their thinking would change if they saw their purpose more along the lines of working with church leadership to create an environment that was inviting for believers and non-believers alike. For example, whatever color they would choose to paint the sanctuary would impact how people felt about worship. This shift in perspective brought new life to the committee. All decisions should ultimately relate to mission, including the use of facilities.

The first principle is that *our interpretation and decisions should lead to bringing God's love to this broken world*. Understandably this is a very broad principle, which immediately raises several other questions, such as "What is meant by God's love?" We will discuss this in due course, but at the start it is imperative that the mission of God be anchored in God's love for this fallen creation and that our decision-making be conducted with this goal in mind.

Therefore, we must continually ask, "Does our use of Scripture and our decisions lead to bringing God's love to a broken world?"

The Centrality of Mission

Christopher J. H. Wright aptly begins his first chapter in *The Mission of God* with, "There are more than enough books offering biblical foundations for Christian mission."[66] This growing area of scholarly and popular study highlights the increasing importance of thinking missionally when applying Scripture. It can legitimately be argued that the mission of God is *the* central theme in Scripture. "Scripture is united by one primary pervading purpose: the tracing of God's unfolding plan of redemption. It everywhere assumes that *this God acts coherently and purposefully in history.*"[67] True, but what does this mean, especially when making decisions wherein the Bible is unclear?

While it is not my purpose to define mission—Wright is correct in that mission has been adequately defined—there are aspects of the study of mission which impact our question and need to be addressed here. It is not my intent to engage the concept of contextualization beyond introductory comments, other than to assert that this is one of the core responsibilities of the church. If the Holy Spirit is the ultimate agent who brings the gospel to the nations, then the church is the visible expression of the gospel. "Wherever it happens to be situated, the church is the local particular embodiment of the gospel story. Consequently, contextualization is inherently an *ecclesial* activity."[68]

I agree with Wright's definition of mission: "Fundamentally, our mission (if it is biblically informed and validated) means our committed participation as God's people, at God's invitation and command, in God's own mission within the history of God's world for the redemption of God's creation."[69] So, how does shaping our interpretation and decisions around the mission of God relate to bringing his love to a broken world, apart from the obvious programs to support missions and local outreach?

The Self-revelation of God

Most Christians in evangelical churches are well aware of the concept that God has revealed himself and wants to be known. At the very heart of the good news is that God has spoken and that he has acted on our behalf. This means that what he has to say is trustworthy. But it also means we have something to talk about. At the very center of this self-revelation is of course Jesus himself. Why is this important in our decision-making?

Living like Jesus is an essential aspect of bringing God's love to a broken world. Now, this is not new information to most Christians. However, how we live this out is a constant challenge. I am continually amazed at how little this truth has genuinely influenced Christian behavior in churches the world over. For example, we criticize with anger amidst a disagreement, all the while overlooking the fact that our anger is just as sinful. We feel the freedom to complain even though the Bible is clear that we should not complain. We talk about one another in ways that are not complementary or encouraging even though we know gossip and slander are to be avoided.

If the heart of the gospel is the self-revelation of Jesus, this means that how we portray Jesus in our organizational behavior and decision-making is essential for the world to *experience* a true sense of this good news. Therefore, our interpretations and decisions must conform to the same gospel lived out by Jesus. This is so because the gospel functions as an instrument to bring about salvation (Rom. 1:16–17).

For the gospel to bring about salvation, it must consistently be demonstrated to those inside as well as outside the church that it has credibility. It is far more than a message... it is life. How can the world understand God if they cannot see him in our lives and all that we do? Thus, our interpretations and decisions must demonstrate evidence of our belief in the gospel.

Remember, my premise is that we have freedom to live out the gospel in different ways in differing cultural settings. Kraft's frame-of-reference principle provides helpful insight into why this might be necessary.[70] Since we live in different contexts, we have different frames of reference. As every missionary has learned, these differences often lead to communication problems. In order to overcome these differences, both the "communicator and receptor must be in a position to attach similar meanings" to the language employed.[71] Specifically, sharing a frame of reference involves creating a common understanding in both areas of culture and language.

Regarding miscommunication, this is what happens when churches fail to communicate the gospel in language understood by the people that come through their doors. Too much "Christianese" leaves the visitor confused or misunderstanding the message. Pastors and educators who preach and teach on a regular rotation recognize this challenge and are always looking for language that is both accessible and true to the biblical text. I believe this explains why Paul used different language from epistle to epistle. His audience (social location) changed with each church, requiring different language to capture common Christian theological themes.

But what about common cultural categories? It is in this area that our first principle is critical. *Even in the same locale*, different churches attract different sorts of people with different values. Kraft identifies a way through this by adopting "the receptor's frame of reference" as the sphere in which communication occurs. This means *as much as possible* we need to understand everyone who enters our churches. The more effective we are at learning about the people who come, including their sinful tendencies, then the more we can align our frames of reference. In other words, we are better able to represent Jesus to them in ways *they* understand.

A classic example of this is Jesus himself when he interacted with the Samaritan woman (John 4). The very setting for the story was Jesus entering into uncomfortable territory for a Jewish rabbi and engaging a woman who, by all ancient cultural standards, was unfaithful. In this story, Jesus answered very few of her questions. Rather, he redirected her thinking by exposing new ideas for her. It is fascinating that he exposed her sinfulness for the purpose of generating new hope, all without confronting or shaming her.

This story forces us to engage our presuppositions and prejudices when engaging in evangelistic outreach. Jesus understood that the woman's thoughts were oriented toward her own cultural situation. The situation itself reflects what Kraft refers to when he encourages "communicators... [to] fit their communication into the categories and felt needs of that frame of reference."[72] How different his interaction was with her when compared to his interaction with, for example Zacchaeus where he said very little and did not *directly* expose or confront Zacchaeus through conversation (Luke 19:1–10).

Understanding this principle has led me to spend time consistently with our teenagers one-on-one in non-threatening environments, with the blessing of their parents. My goal is twofold. First, to help them think through the myriad of challenges they face daily. Second, to listen for trends developing within our own local culture. They become my eyes into their generational culture. When I see repeated patterns, I know that I will soon see this same challenge in our church context. This allows me to work with our leadership to begin to form a theological way of thinking *prior to* seeing the challenge manifest itself in our congregation.

For now, the self-revelation of God through his Son Jesus provides a model for how to begin using Scripture to shape our individual church cultures. It is important that our interpretation of Scripture and decision-making take these freedoms into account if we are to effectively reach the vast majority of people who do not think like we do and who do not share our "frames of reference." For those of you beginning to fear that we are slipping our theological moorings, be patient. There are controls coming that will continue to anchor us in orthodoxy.

God's Diversified Creation

Let us take a further look at diversity and wrestle with the question of why God made us different in the first place. Cultural homogeneity is not a key feature of Christianity.[73] Rather, Christianity must display more cultural diversity than any other religion. This is obvious as the Scriptures unfold in their expression of mission.

From the very beginning of the Scriptures, diversity appears, starting with gender diversity (Gen. 1–2). The table of nations and the story of Babel reveal several things regarding the mission of God (Gen. 10–11). In particular, the story of Babel raises, with intensity, the question of how diversity relates to God's plan. God had told Noah and his family to "be fruitful and increase in number and fill the earth" (Gen. 9:1, 7). Genesis 11 demonstrates that humanity had failed to act on that command. This resulted in direct intervention by God to disperse the nations as he had commanded (Gen. 11:8–9).[74] The intervention by God at Babel was so violent and sudden that they could no longer stay together, but were forced to separate and, therefore, diversify.

This story reveals that one of the common building blocks of human culture is the ability to communicate (Gen. 11:1). But, as with many corruptions resulting from the fall, this story also reveals that culture develops primarily *for the purpose of survival* (Gen. 11:2–4). Humanity develops those *behaviors* which are believed to ensure ongoing existence. For example, they developed the necessary building materials and technology to build a city and, therefore, carry out their drive for self-preservation. The intervention by God assured the greater division socially, geographically, physically, culturally, and politically. In effect, the "confusion of languages prevents community living and technological cooperation: people cannot trust or work with those they do not understand."[75] This divine act of confusing the languages and dispersing the peoples further solidified the ethnic diversity identified in Genesis 10.

24

The call to Abram and the promise to bless him, his family, and the nations (Gen. 12) are presented against the backdrop of this establishment of various cultures. With Abram, God begins systematically to act to bring redemption to humanity. God creates diversity and then chooses one from the many to reach the many. "Israel came into existence as a people with a mission entrusted to them from God for the sake of God's wider purpose of blessing the nations."[76]

I believe this is God's design and gives insight into why God created differing cultures as discussed in Chapter 1. It is anthropological in nature. In other words, different cultural settings allow diverse ways of understanding *and experiencing* the gospel. God becomes "three-dimensional" as we listen to different cultures. This is because each culture has different language and practices that enable them to conceptualize and live out the gospel within their own frame of reference. When cultures listen to each other, then God becomes more accessible and alive to us. Another way of saying this is, God cannot be fully known until all ethnicities have spoken. This is what happens in the future when "persons from every tribe and language and people and nation" are together praising God (Rev. 5:9).

Thus, our diversity becomes the means by which we can contrast and compare the truth of Christianity. As discussed above, this can only happen as we get better at aligning our experiences and creating a more common frame of reference. This is captured well by Paul's statements about becoming all things to all people (1 Cor. 9:19–23). As Blomberg is quick to remind us, Paul is not promoting pure situational ethics nor is he applying this strategy to every area of life. "He does not assume that all aspects of culture are inherently evil but practices what has come to be called the contextualization of the gospel—changing the *forms* of the message precisely to preserve its *content*."[77]

An example of this is sharing fellowship at meals. Many of my Christian friends in India have taught me that the proper way for them to show respect for their non-believing friends is to wait on, but not sit at, the table when they invite guests to dinner. To eat together would be culturally offensive. Conversely, when I am there we eat together. This, and many other examples, has convinced me that we have freedom to live out the gospel in different ways. This will have greater impact later in the study as we look at the various ways people sin in any given church context and discuss how to engage them about their sin.

For now, it is important to understand that we have freedom and should exercise that freedom to bring God's love to this world. God's purpose in creating diversity is that we might together come to know him better. It is precisely through our *differences* that we can come to a fuller and richer understanding of him.

In the church context this emphasis on diversity and mission becomes very important for several reasons, *even if the local culture reflects little ethnic diversity*. First, diversity actually does occur within each church in several other areas, such as differences in generations, politics, socio-economic status, experience, struggles with sin, and so on. Understanding how diversity functions and how the stories of Scripture navigated those diverse situations, all for the purpose of mission, provides models for managing diversity in the local church.

Second, the story of the Gentiles coming into the church and how leadership responded provides an example of how to engage people who are different in their culture, ethnicity, and *even their sinful patterns*. The stories discussed earlier of Cornelius (Acts 10–11) and the Gentile new believers (Acts 15) reveal the natural tendency for groups to survive. It is very challenging to welcome diversity, in all of its aspects, into a church with established relational and organizational patterns. For most pastors this is a common as well as complex problem.

Finally, it is common knowledge that most people feel more comfortable with people like them. Even when our churches work to diversify, typically that means that one group must become more or less like another group. This becomes especially significant when we "welcome" people struggling with sin with which we are particularly uncomfortable.[78] How do we allow for diversity regarding sin while still creating a redemptive culture? More on this in the next chapter.

26

The Authority of Scripture

Jumping ahead, the Great Commission implies a mandate for the people of God (Matt. 28:18–20). And yet, it does much more. It reveals that our obedience falls under the authority of Scripture. In order to more precisely define what we mean by mission, it is helpful to first address the question of authority. Specifically, what is the purpose of Scripture?[79] It is not a list of rules, nor a listing of true doctrines. It is also not a means of exercising control over a people.[80] Church history is full of examples wherein churches which overuse the phrase "the Bible says..." often experience division or conflict, as some read it one way and others read it another way. Similarly, it is not primarily a devotional aid, although it has much in it that aids in our spiritual devotions. Those churches who have "heard God" through Scripture tend to be those where division is most apparent.[81] Finally it is not a "happy book"—if we only obey it, we will be happy.[82]

So, what is it? It is primarily a story,[83] but how can a story have authority? As discussed earlier, Jesus used narrative (the story of David) to answer the legal questions put forth by the Jewish leadership. This suggests that the narrative (descriptive) sections of Scripture carry as much weight as the prescriptive sections. In my experience, this is not how many Christians think. In the classroom, as well as in the church (no matter the country), authority is most often seen as expressed with the imperatives. The problem with this approach is that an emphasis on the imperatives overlooks the vast majority of Scripture.

Therefore, it is necessary to have a healthy working understanding of how Scripture functions authoritatively. When we refer to authority, it is shorthand for the authority of God as exercised through Scripture. The narrative portions of Scripture reveal the *experiences* of the people of God throughout the history of the Bible as God demonstrates his authority and his people respond to that authority. This was part of the decision-making process utilized by the apostles at the Jerusalem

Council as they reflected back on their experiences and developed solutions from those experiences.

The Great Commission reveals more than simply God's plan to reach the entire world. It also captures the experience and ministry of Jesus himself. In this regard, it represents what *should be* the orthopraxis of the church.[84] I am distinguishing practice from praxis here. *Practice* has more to do with behavior, which may or may not embody the truths of Christianity. In contrast, *praxis* is a set of behaviors wherein the *telos* (end goal) itself is captured in the behavior. Moving a congregation to praxis is much more challenging and requires more patience and planning than simply emphasizing practice and behavior.

This means that the Great Commission should be embodied in the very life of the members of any church *and the decision-making of their leadership*, which includes all policies, procedures, ministries, board decisions, preaching, worship function, and so on. The Great Commission is missiological in that it represents the end goal of our responsibility; making disciples of all the nations and *teaching* them to observe Jesus' teaching. Wright has helpfully defined mission in the more general sense as "a long-term purpose or goal that is to be achieved through proximate objectives and planned actions."[85] This should *overtly* drive all interpretation of Scripture as challenges are identified and solutions developed.

A New Paradigm: Love

Back to the concept of God's love and the risks of misinterpreting this important area. In his opening paragraph, Gerald Bray states, "God is love. Everything we know about him teaches us that, and every encounter we have with him expresses it. God's love for us is deep and all-embracing, but it is not the warmhearted sentimentality that often goes by the name of love today."[86] With this opening statement, Bray lays out the foundational statement which shapes his systematic theology, with the appropriate caution that we properly understand God's love.

It would be easy, in today's world, to understand our first principle in ways that are contrary to Scripture. I have been asked many times, for example, "What's wrong with friends with benefits if we *love* each other?" This highlights the importance of carefully defining the concept of God's love in keeping with the Scriptures.

When the Bible claims that God is love (1 John 4:18), to what specifically is it referring? As Bray argues, "The love which the Bible speaks about is not a self-centered kind of preening in the mirror, but a concern for others... The love of the Father for the Son and the corresponding love of the Son for his Father are best understood, not as a conceptual act inside the mind of God but as the kind of self-sacrifice that characterizes the relationship of one person to another."[87]

This is an important distinction that begins to identify appropriate boundaries of what love is and is not. Love is not the freedom to do whatever one wishes! Christianity has long recognized and agreed that God's love is best displayed to us by what Jesus did on the cross (John 3:16; Rom. 5:8; Gal. 2:20; 1 John 4:10). This other-centered, self-sacrifice of Jesus helps shape the contours of how we define and express love in any particular context. In other words, to ask what is the loving thing to do does not always mean what brings the greatest happiness or pleasure in the moment to the one being loved (as any parent will attest). The action of love needs to be shaped by the needs in the present situation. In other words, love in the biblical sense is always framed according to the needs of the person requiring the love.[88]

At the church in Nepal where I have preached for many years, I have often been brought to tears as they take their offering. Many of the people are very poor, but as they come in to church, they each bring a "tithe" of rice! By the time church starts, they usually have to carry several vats of rice to the front wherein the elders pray over the rice and ask God's blessing as they distribute it to needy people... both to believers and non-believers. This is love.

The Importance of Obedience within the Framework of Love

When challenged by the Pharisees, it is intriguing that Jesus summarized the law in the language of love (Matt. 22:34–40). His reference to Deuteronomy 6:5 and Leviticus 19:18 identified the thread that tied the law together: love. In my experience, most Christians have never read the law, yet they have come to the conclusion that the law was impossible to keep.[89] A reading of the law reveals that it was neither ambiguous nor impossible. Each command was clear and easy to obey for any individual Israelite. As Paul argued, what made it impossible was not the law itself, but our own sinful hearts. This is why he could portray the law in very positive terms (Rom. 7:7–12).

Jesus goes one step further and claims, "All the Law and the Prophets hang on these two commandments" (Matt. 22:40). This is a way of saying that the commandments of the law and the teaching of the prophets cannot be fulfilled apart from the twofold love commandment. In other words, these two commands provide a deeper understanding of the purpose of the law.

This background helps us understand Jesus' actions and teachings on obedience. During his final night with the disciples before he was crucified, he left them with teachings that would change their lives and the church forever. He began with the symbolic action of washing his disciples' feet (John 13:2–17). After Judas left, he went further and anchored his actions in love with the famous verse, "A new command I give you: Love one another. As I have loved you, so you must love one another. By this everyone will know that you are my disciples, if you love one another" (John 13:34–35).

But he does not stop there. As he moves more deeply into his final teachings, he ties love and obedience together. "If you love me, keep my commands" (John 14:15). This is in the context of sending the promised Holy Spirit. John Oswalt has observed that when Jesus spoke of the promise of the Father (Luke 24:49)—the sending of the Spirit—the disciples did not question him. This was out of character as they seemed to question him regarding every aspect of his messiahship.[90] Perhaps this is because he finally said something they expected the Messiah to say. This same observation applies to his teaching about the Spirit in John 14.

The very heart of the New Covenant was the sending of the Spirit. Jeremiah prophesied that the New Covenant would essentially include creating a new heart within God's people, specifically by God writing his law upon the hearts of his people (Jer. 31:33–34). Ezekiel further prophesied that the New Covenant would result in cleansing God's people and replacing their heart of stone with hearts of flesh (Ezek. 36:24–26). He adds that this would occur by the indwelling Spirit of God (Ezek. 36:27–30). In Ezekiel 37:1–14, the parable of the dry bones created a further vivid image of what life in the Spirit would be like. In other words, the Spirit would cleanse as well as bring life (John 6:63).

Further, one of the primary marks of the Messiah was that he was a man upon whom the Spirit would rest and who would proclaim a message of hope and new life. Early in the ministry of Jesus, he quoted Isaiah 61:1–3 in his own hometown, essentially asserting that the prophecy of the Spirit resting on him had been accomplished (Luke 4:18–19; John 3:34–35). Jesus' use of this passage demonstrated a core message that the Messiah would bring freedom for the prisoners. "In fact, the totality of the deliverance that Isaiah described is now put into motion with Jesus' coming. He is the Servant *par excellence*."[91] In other words, the time of deliverance for humanity had come.

This is the background to Jesus' teachings in John 14 concerning the relationship between obedience, love, and the Holy Spirit. All three come together to help us understand what life is now like under the New Covenant. Jesus had just surprised the disciples by claiming that they would be doing greater things than he had done, precisely because he was going to the Father (John 14:12). This sets the stage for his promise that the Father would send "another advocate" who is identified as the Spirit (John 14:16–17). It is the coming Spirit that enables believers to do greater things, *including redemptive engagement with those struggling with sin*! And sandwiched in between these two ideas is the notion that loving Jesus leads to keeping his commands.[92] In fact, it is the keeping of the commands that reveals whether Jesus' teaching actually comes from God or not (John 7:17).

Now we can grasp the true nature of the New Covenant and how it relates to mission in John 13–14. Jesus began by demonstrating his love for his disciples by washing their feet, followed by teaching them about the deeper relationship with the Father, his astounding statement about them doing greater things than he had done, and now his linking together their love (made possible by the Spirit) with obedience. This surprising cascade of his example followed by his teachings brings all of the strands of the New Covenant passages together: cleansing by the Spirit, replacing the old heart with a new one capable of loving, embedding his law—his teachings—in this new heart, and replacing the old motivation with a new one. These breathtaking last words of Jesus clearly illustrate release from sin and spiritual captivity. A new day has dawned.

One more critical truth is surfaced in John 14:21, "The one who loves me will be loved by my Father, and I too will love them and show myself to them." "The groundwork is being laid for the 'oneness' between Jesus and his disciples that mirrors the oneness between Jesus and his heavenly Father."[93] A significant goal within the spiritual formation movement is to more clearly experience and understand Christ. In this passage, Jesus made it clear that obedience, motivated by love and empowered by the Spirit, is the key that brings him into the life of a person and community in more deep and intimate ways.

When love is defined in terms of obedience, certain aspects of church life become clearer. It seems to me that churches are increasingly struggling to identify sin as sin and deal with it appropriately. Rather, the tendency seems to be either to "lower the bar," all with good intention, or confront sin and demand obedience in order to deal with it quickly. It does not help when churches either "normalize" sin or create unwelcome environments. Grace is not the same as "anything goes." Paul responded to this approach in 1 Corinthians 6:12–20 regarding sexual immorality. His conclusion was to flee from sexual immorality.

Once normalized, sin is no longer in need of redemption. Similarly, when ostracized, those who are struggling will find little actual help in the church, and certainly not in the world either. It is helpful to ask the question of today's churches, "Why do people come?" Any pastor who knows their flock realizes that their people come to church carrying a variety of heavy burdens including the task of enduring the challenges of life. I believe the primary reason people come to church *in today's world* is the genuine belief that there is something better than what they are experiencing. Why else come? Failure to deliver on that genuine desire for a better life is perhaps one of most harmful things a church can do.

The very best thing that we can do in the church is help people learn to authentically love and trust God and obey him. Conversely, one of the devastating things we can do is to fail to effectively engage sin in *loving and redemptive* ways. In my experience, more often than not, this failure creates a very unhealthy environment and pushes people away from the heart of the gospel. This is missional thinking in that *everything* we do should lead to effectively loving others in the midst of their sin and guiding them to a deeper love of God along with a growing desire to live holy lives!

Summary

If we understand that the mission of God is central to all that the church does, then several other implications follow. First, the example of God revealing himself in his Son gives us a model of how we are to act toward others. All that the Son did was for the purpose of glorifying his Father and bringing about redemption in this fallen world. This should guide our thinking as we develop our philosophies of ministry, our policies and procedures, and our ministry practices.

Second, God's creation of diversity provides for a more natural means by which he can come to be known among his people. If we are willing to embrace, and even celebrate this diversity we are setting our congregations up for experiences that go beyond their normal lives. However, this is not restricted to ethnic diversity. Diversity comes in many forms, including the individual ways in which people struggle with sin and express it in their lives.

Third, the Great Commission provides the marching orders for the church as well as giving us the contours of what praxis should look like. Simultaneously, it allows for the authority of Scripture to be captured in the narrative stories as well as the prescriptive teachings of Jesus. This was the example followed by the Jerusalem Council when wrestling through integrating Gentile believers into the church.

Finally, with the New Covenant comes a new paradigm; love should be the core motivation to move into the lives of our people, both inside and outside the church. With the coming of the Spirit into our lives, it is now possible and expected that our obedience will be motivated by and expressed in this deep and growing love.

What this means is that all of our interpretations and decisions should lead to bringing God's love out to this broken world. Remember, in our decision-making model, we are considering both the Spirit-led informed intuition of the group while at the same time looking at multiple possible decisions based on our interpretation of various passages. This first principle provides the first step in our interpretive framework by ensuring that all decisions fit within the mission of God. If our practices, rituals, traditions, and behaviors as a church do not lead to this result, we should check our interpretation.

Chapter 3

ENGAGING OUR CULTURE WITH CHRISTIAN ETHICS

S oon after I assumed the role of Senior Pastor, we had a situation involving a person in our fellowship who was struggling deeply with sin. The elders asked about my approach to helping this person. I responded that, before I answered I first needed to know the rate at which they expected redemption to occur. For example, would they be pleased if a drug addict overcame their addiction within one week? With a chuckle they responded, "Of course!" How about a year? "Absolutely!" How about 10 years... lots of head scratches. How about a lifetime? Expectations regarding redemption are complex and involve time. There is a difference between deciding to apply the Bible and the manner in which the Bible is applied.

The second principle is that *our interpretation and decisions should lead to redemption in our current cultural setting.* Just because the Bible specifies a behavior does not mean it must be followed in the precise way commanded. Church history is replete with examples of biblical imperatives and practices that are either no longer applicable or have been lived out in ways different than their original setting. The very nature of this book is to present the guidelines that help us make these sorts of decisions. This is critical if, for no other reason, than to help the surrounding culture understand why we do what we do. Our decisions must lead to redemption (or health) in our current cultural setting. In this chapter, we are answering the question, "Does our interpretation and decisions lead to redemption in our current cultural setting?"

In order to effectively engage culture with what we believe about right and wrong, we must first grasp several key theological concepts. What is meant by redemption? In the church and the classroom rarely do I have someone who can discuss this concept beyond the true, but inadequate fact, that we have been redeemed in Christ. Why do we still struggle with sin and what actually is sin beyond "missing the mark?" If we have the Holy Spirit does this mean we still sin or not and what role does the Spirit play? If we are part of the new creation, why do we still struggle so greatly? Finally, how are we to engage with our people in such a way that these theological concepts become life-giving?

The Challenge of Theology

I began this chapter by referring to these areas as theological concepts. This is because for most Christians, this is all that they are... concepts. It may be that we have done the church a disservice by communicating these truths in individualistic, personal, and static ways. This may be behind David Wells' charge, "When the word *theology* is used in the Church, it is commonly used simply of someone's private theory about some subject."[94]

To illustrate the risk associated with this, if a parent teaches their child from the beginning of life until they leave for college that integrity is important, yet they fail to live a life of integrity, which will have the greater impact in the longer span of the child's life? To be sure, it is our modeling demonstrated by the way we live our lives.[95] This pitfall is addressed in many parenting models where parents learn that values are "caught" by their children, rather than taught. Is it even possible to teach the deeper values that the Bible is concerned about? How do you "teach" what a good marriage is? It must be experienced *first*.[96] This has tremendous impact in hermeneutics. The relationship between experience, behavior, and biblical principles is symbiotic in that they depend on each other.[97]

Similar to parenting, where in the church are our doctrinal statements lived out in ways that connect with the lives of our members? Wells' point is well-founded in that many in our church can only express theology in terms of concepts, if at all. Even our discussions and definitions about theology often appear technical and static; that is the strength of higher education. Craig Keener, in discussing experiential reading, defines it as "believing to the depths of our being what we find in the text. For example, it is one thing to affirm academically that God loves us. It is another to welcome that truth into our hearts that have felt wounded and untrusting."[98] If Christians struggle to bring theology into their own experiences in life-giving ways, how can we expect them to transfer those wonderful truths to their own cultural setting?

At this point, it might be helpful to think of theology as a conversation about God. It is true that when we discuss theology we are thinking systematically about the fundamental ideas of Christianity. But it is so much more than that; it should also be a discussion about all aspects of our lives and knowledge of God, and generate conversation for all who live and breathe, who wrestle and fear, hope and pray. It should be a study about God in the community of faith and be something that we learn about, sing about, preach on, reflect on, celebrate, and engage as a community of faith. It should be a conversation that takes place between family members about what it means to behold the one, true living God. Every discussion we have about God should create thriving, energetic conversations. With this in mind, let us jump into the concept of sin and redemption, and how they are actually connected to all that we do.

The Nature of Sin

Before developing redemptive approaches to sin, it is necessary first to develop a working understanding of sin. At some level, every Christian understands sin as they deal with it constantly. However, in my experience, most Christians (including church leaders) see sin simply as the breaking of a moral code. While true, this view is inadequate both theologically and pastorally, and has often led to ineffective and destructive strategies in approaching people struggling with sin.[99]

This raises the parallel question of how most Christians view God. Do they see God as a giant tyrant in the sky with a list of rules and regulations? Or do they see God as the one, true living God, who created us for deep joy and identified as sin anything that would rob us of that joy? Sadly, my experience says that most Christians and non-Christians alike, in our modern culture, view God from the first perspective! This requires that we develop a healthier view of sin before working to address it in the church context. This is especially critical as the complexity and unique approaches to sin are coming into our churches in more increasing and transparent ways.

The terminology for sin is "extensive, numbering more than forty words."[100] This points to the importance of this subject. We all know from experience that something is horribly wrong in the relationship between us and God, and between each other.

The wisdom literature of the Old Testament is helpful at this point as this literature seeks to help us navigate the challenges of life. For example, Proverbs give us a set of metaphors for understanding sin and the two pathways that one can travel: the way of wisdom and the way of folly. The one who takes the proper way is shown to be wise, while the one to takes the pathway of folly is shown to be a fool.

While the study of wisdom is widely discussed and debated, for our purposes we can draw a simple conclusion: one has choices in life. One can choose the road of wisdom or the road of foolishness. This is captured in Proverbs 1:20–33 where wisdom calls to whomever will listen to choose the wise path. The wise are prudent and have good sense to do what is right and just and fair (Prov. 1:4–4), show discretion in their life and in their planning (Prov. 2:11), and demonstrate insight and act sensibly (Prov. 1:5). In contrast, the foolish person is gullible (Prov. 1:10), arrogant and does not need council (Prov. 12:15), has contempt for wisdom (Prov. 1:7), is a mocker (Prov. 1:22), and has no sense (Prov. 7:7).

For pastors and others who work regularly with people who struggle with sin, this picture accurately describes what sin does to a person and to relationships. They are typically either enjoying freedom and joy or entrapment and struggle. Why the difference? Why don't they all struggle? More on this shortly. With this picture of wisdom and foolishness in mind, let us consider sin a little more pastorally.

Sin by definition is ubiquitous in that it pervades all of human existence. And yet, as Michael Bird accurately claims, "It's hard to be precise [about sin] because there is a plethora of images for sin in Scripture."[101] For our purposes, let's narrow down this broad area to a working definition. Cornelius Plantinga has given us a helpful start. "Let us say that a sin is any act—any thought, desire, emotion, word, or deed—or its particular absence, that displeases God and deserves blame... God hates sin not just because it violates his law but, more substantively, because *it violates shalom*, because it breaks the peace, because it interferes with the way things are supposed to be... In fact, we may safely describe evil as any spoiling of shalom, whether physically (e.g., by disease), morally, spiritually, or otherwise."[102]

It is the aspect of breaking shalom (peace) that is important for our study. What is shalom? It is a very rich concept that at its heart has the idea of peace. And it is far more than the absence of conflict. When you look at the various aspects of shalom in the Old Testament, "It is a state of positive friendship and security between two parties, often the result of restitution and reconciliation."[103] This gives us a glimpse of the destructiveness of sin. It is a fracture between relationships which robs us of life and is an obstacle to the way things are supposed to be. So, how does sin break shalom?

First, at the most basic theological level sin is "missing the mark." What mark? In the ancient Greek world sin was viewed as a serious offense against a deity. Offense for what? The answer to these questions will immediately shape a congregation's view of sin and how to address it at a pastoral level. A key that many overlook relates to our fundamental purpose for being created. Genesis 1:26–28 (cf, Gen. 2:15) informs us that one of our primary purposes for being created was to "rule over" creation. In other words, we are to work together in relationship and enjoy creation which will lead to the joy that God intended. When we fulfill our God-created purpose of taking care of creation, *which includes each other*, this brings us great joy.

Paul, in Romans 1:18–32 identifies our key sin as reversing the process. Rather than caring for and serving creation, humanity began to worship creation. This was the one thing we were not permitted to do. We began to worship "birds and animals and reptiles" (Rom. 1:23). We then began to worship "created things" (Rom. 1:25). We then ultimately began to worship our own bodies, rather than serve each other and God (Rom. 1:26–27). At its core, this is idolatry. All sin should be viewed in this context (Rom. 1:28–32). Idolatry is simply worshiping something other than God. In other words, we have "missed the mark" identified by God.[104]

Second, at a personal level sin should be viewed as an obstacle. An obstacle to what? If sin is an obstacle, this implies that we are moving toward something and sin blocks that process. The ultimate goal is that we are being transformed into the image of Christ (2 Cor. 3:17–18). These words are very familiar to Christians, but often with very little depth of understanding. What does this mean? At a practical level it means we are being transformed into the type of human seen and experienced in the Person of Christ… a true human. In other words, we are becoming more loving, gracious, generous, affectionate, sacrificial, servant-oriented, and so on.[105]

Sin blocks this process. As the New Testament clarifies, sin prevents people from developing as God intends.[106] This should re-envision the way we view sin. If a parent does not tell their young child that they cannot play in the street because they could get hurt, the child might still get hurt by going into the street. Therefore, it is an act of grace for the parent to tell the child the truth. It is no different with God. If God had not told us that alcoholism was a sin, it would still be destructive. Our only way of discovering the destructiveness of alcoholism would be to experience it first-hand. Therefore, it is an act of grace that God revealed alcoholism to be sin. God is not trying to control us. No, he is trying to protect us!

From a pastoral perspective, this is how personal sin should be viewed in the church context. It is not a list of rules, but rather the behaviors and thinking that move us from caring for creation and each other to idolatry—serving ourselves—all of which robs us of joy and is an affront to the one true living God. Therefore, the question we should be asking is not what sin is being committed, but what is the impact to the sinning person, how is that sin impeding their movement toward Christ (true humanity), and how is it bringing destruction in their other relationships?[107] The picture of restored shalom is captured beautifully in the priestly blessing: "The Lord bless you and keep you; the Lord make his face to shine on you and be gracious to you; the Lord turn his face toward you and give you peace (shalom)" (Num. 6:24–26).

The Nature of Redemption

Now we are ready to address the concept of redemptive cultures. First, let us clarify the concept of redemption. The study of redemption is a vast area of study. At its core, it has to do with God acting through his covenant promises to draw his people from being in Adam to being in Christ. This is typically referred to as redemptive history or similar language. Many evangelical Christians are familiar with this concept.

For the purposes of this study, I want to look more closely at what it means to be redemptive in relationships. This is a rich concept with deep roots in the Old Testament. This concept is first found in the exodus story. Martens has persuasively argued that Exodus 5:22–6:8 "clarifies the way in which the central subject of the Old Testament, Yahweh, is to be elaborated. Yahweh has a plan. This plan is one to bring deliverance, to summon a people who will be peculiarly his own, to offer himself for them to know and to give them land in fulfillment of his promise."[108]

In this account, Moses had just come from Pharaoh where he had been asked the crucial question, "Who is the Lord, that I should obey him and let Israel go? I do not know the Lord and I will not let Israel go" (Exod. 5:2). Moses went back to the Lord to learn what he was up to (Exod. 5:22–23). God's response spelled out his design for all of redemptive history and laid a foundation for what it means for our churches to develop redemptive cultures.

God began by reminding Moses that he is Yahweh and that he appeared to the Patriarchs as God Almighty (Exod. 6:2–5). His self-revelation to the Patriarchs was for the purpose of establishing his covenant with them. This covenant formed the basis for his redemptive plan. This introduction was significant because it reminded Moses that God is the God of the living, it established historical continuity by reviewing the past, and it provided theological continuity by connecting the divine name with the name God Almighty.[109]

This is the context in which God laid out his plan to *redeem* the Israelites from slavery (Exod. 6:6). He further explained that they would become his prized possession, that they would have a relationship with him, and that he would give them a gift of land (Exod. 6:7–8). This is where we get the idea of being saved, or rescued, in the more popular use of that idea. The exodus event is therefore redemptive at its heart.

As many word studies have demonstrated, this term—redemption, redeem—is crucial in biblical history and means simply to help another who is in trouble and is powerless to help themselves. Sandra Richter argues that "the concept of redemption actually entered the Bible through the laws and mores of Israel's patriarchal, tribal culture. Specifically, the idea of redemption was intrinsically linked to the familial responsibilities of a patriarch to his clan."[110] Wright refers to this as "a metaphor drawn from the social and economic life of Israel."[111] It is used, for example, of those in financial trouble as well as those who are enslaved. A redeemer then was one who acted "as protector, defender, avenger or rescuer for other members of the family, especially in situations of threat, loss, poverty, or injustice. Such action would always involve effort, often incurred cost, and sometimes demanded a degree of self-sacrifice." [112]

Perhaps the best-known illustration of redemption is found in the book of Ruth. Right from the beginning the book of Ruth is clear that the problem is related to the death, pain, and emptiness that has afflicted the life of Naomi. In summary, as the story unfolds Naomi returned to Bethlehem with her daughter-in-law, Ruth, after her husband and two sons died. Through a series of events, Ruth met a relative, Boaz, who married her and restored her and Naomi's honor. The outcome was that Ruth and Boaz became the grandparents of David. Boaz's role was a significant part of the main theme, which includes "the kindness, graciousness, and sagacity of Boaz, expressed in his benevolence and his faithfulness to family responsibilities, in regard to marrying Ruth the Moabitess and to redeeming the field of Elimelech on behalf of Naomi, all of which transcended the claims of self-interest." [113]

In this story, two well-known ideas surface related to the concept of redemption. The first is related to the role of Boaz. He is described by Ruth as a "guardian-redeemer" (Ruth 3:9, go'el [114]). This was a legal term to describe one who had the obligation to care for a relative in serious trouble. "A go'el was any member within a wider family group upon whom fell the duty of acting to protect the interests of the family or another member in it who was in particular need." [115]

Second, when this word is combined with the concept of loving-kindness (hesed) discussed earlier, we begin to see what authentic redemption looks like. Naomi's wish for her daughters-in-law was that the Lord would show them the same kindness (hesed) that they had demonstrated toward their husbands (Ruth 1:8). Indeed, Ruth's well-known response to go with Naomi is an example of that deep commitment that Naomi had observed (Ruth 1:16–17). This is then reciprocated by Boaz in his care for these women in that he had not stopped showing kindness (hesed, Ruth 2:20). Finally, Boaz recognized that Ruth herself was demonstrating kindness (*hesed*) by her loyalty both to Naomi, and then to Boaz by not pursuing younger men (Ruth 3:10). The *combination* of commitment with deep devotion provides a clear picture of one of the key dynamics that should define any church environment.

Herein lies some of the power when creating a redemptive and loving environment. The story of Ruth models the truth that God uses the faithfulness of ordinary people to do great things. Ruth also illustrates that behind the human endeavor is the all-powerful love of God himself. This is captured in the end of the story in that their faithfulness eventually led to David's birth (Ruth 4:18–22). This is why the psalmist could cry out repeatedly that God's love (*hesed*) would endure forever (Ps. 118:1–4). David is evidence that this story is also about God's love and care for Israel.[116] When we truly understand what it means for God *and us* to be redemptive, then other parts of the story of redemption come alive and help us make sense of church life.

Priests and Sacrifices

This raises the question of the role that *we* play in the redemptive process. It is no accident that both Paul and Peter use the metaphors priest and sacrifice to describe church life. Rituals are symbolic by nature. They are designed to shape the beliefs and views of reality within people groups.[117] These two metaphors are no different. Understanding how they function is vital to understanding what a redemptive culture looks like as well as how to establish this type of culture. Since these two metaphors are bound to the ancient culture, let us take a brief look at the Old Testament concept behind each metaphor and actions associated with each.

Priesthood. The priests had several functions of which three are important for our study.[118] First, they were to represent God to the people (Lev. 10:11). The people would come to know God through the teachings of the priests. Second, they were to bring the people to God

(Lev. 1–7). This was accomplished through bringing their sacrifices forward. Third, they were to bless the people (Num. 6:22–27).

The combination of these three actions represents the heart of what it means to mediate for another. Put in the context of the Ancient Near East, these three actions communicated the relationship as well as the attitudes defining the relationship. The gods of the ancient world were to be placated more than emulated. In Israel's culture, the one true God wanted more than their worship. He wanted them to be like him and enjoy him in relationship. This was one of the primary tasks of the priesthood.

This is the background for understanding God's first offer of covenant to Israel after they had come out of Egypt. They were standing at the base of Mt. Sinai. They had witnessed the ten plagues against the gods of Egypt, had sung the song of celebration of Moses, had witnessed God delivering water and manna, and now it was time to personally meet him (Exod. 19:3–6).

This passage defines the identity and role of Israel in God's mission.[119] God first reminded them of his redemption and rescue of them from the Egyptians. And then he made his offer of covenant. The result of their obedience would be to become God's treasured possession. But, more than that, they would become his priests.

This was a remarkable statement to go from slaves to priests! And even more remarkable was that it would be hereditary. In Egypt, for example, priests served for a limited time before returning to their normal occupations. In contrast, in Mesopotamia, priests were appointed by the king.[120] Limiting the priesthood to the Aaronic line put Israel in a unique position that was radically different than their neighbors. Since the priests had to exemplify the concept of holiness (Lev. 21), they became a model for the Israelites to see what it meant to be priests.

This raises the question, to whom were they to mediate? Following the promise to Abraham (Gen. 12:1–3) and God's own contextualizing of the covenant offer in terms of the "whole earth" (Exod. 19:5), the implication is clear. They would become his priests to the rest of the nations. They were to bring the redemption they had experienced to the rest of the world.

In a stunning way, Peter uses this very verse to show that the church has now assumed the role originally given to Israel (1 Pet. 2:9–10). This allows us to better grasp what our function is in carrying out the mission of God. We are to be priests to the nations, and we are to fulfill this responsibility in a redemptive manner. Karen Jobes emphasizes this with a further important point. This passage is not focused on the individual believer. In the ancient world the priesthood was set apart for ministry to their deity. As we just saw, Israel was set apart *as a nation to reach the nations.* "Peter now declares similarly that collectively Christian believers are to perform that same function with respect to the nations."[121]

Interpreting the Scriptures with a community in view, rather than an individual, is one of the central aspects of our principle in this chapter. Our morality, as expressed through our behaviors, must be demonstrated in community settings as churches. I have seen many believers and churches wherein this is largely emphasized at the individual level. I agree that it starts at the individual level, but it is not ultimately fulfilled until expressed in relationship and community. One may decide to love others, but how can they fulfill this command if there is no one to love? This is the fundamental weakness for those in my community who say, "I can find God in the mountains!" True, but it requires community to fulfill the very heart of redemption.[122]

As a short aside, a reading of the Historical Books and the Prophets reveals that the failure of the priesthood was one of the primary causes of God's intense judgements and, ultimately, the exile of the nation. This should cause churches to pause and intentionally ask the question of whether or not they are fulfilling the functions of the priesthood in their local communities.

Sacrifice. When we turn to sacrifice, we see a similar pattern developed. As argued earlier, rituals are symbolic by nature. They are designed to shape the beliefs and views of reality within people groups. Therefore, it is not surprising that sacrificial language is interwoven throughout the church in almost every culture. This makes it familiar. At another level, its commonality means that the theology behind the Christian concept of sacrifice is somewhat marginalized and inadequate.[123] In my experience, most Christians are appropriately familiar with the sacrifice of Christ, and possibly the concept of sacrifice in the season of Lent, but are very unfamiliar with the metaphor as it relates to church life.

While sacrifice was an integral part of the ancient world, for the Christian the obvious starting point is the sacrificial system found in Leviticus 1–7. While the sacrificial system provided a means of approaching the Lord in his tabernacle, the sacrifices also functioned to maintain the relationship with God by preserving purity and holiness of both the tabernacle and the community. They did this through sacrificial rituals which were physical actions designed to capture the experience of surfacing sin, thanksgiving, and so on. For our purposes, the Old Testament represents sacrifice most of all as giving something costly to God.

When we turn to the New Testament, we see both Peter and Paul bringing the concept of sacrifice into the church. In 1 Peter 2:4–5 Peter brings both metaphors of priesthood and sacrifice together. The community is to fulfill their priestly responsibilities by together offering spiritual sacrifices. There is much discussion over what specifically constitutes a spiritual sacrifice. What we can say with confidence it that these are sacrifices that God desires (1 Pet. 2:5).

As discussed above, the church now has the responsibility of serving as priests (1 Pet. 2:9–10). In this passage we have a clue as to what God desires. The church has become a priesthood *for the specific purpose* of declaring the praises of God who redeemed us. Declaring these praises to whom? I would argue that our praises are for the purposes of encouraging those within as well as attracting those outside of the church. Peter had just urged his readers to "have sincere love for each other" and to "love one another deeply, from the heart" (1 Pet. 1:22). Following his discussion of priesthood he further urges his readers to "live such good lives among the pagans that, though they accuse you of doing wrong, they may see your good deeds and glorify God on the day he visits us" (1 Pet. 2:12).

This pattern of attracting the outside world is consistent throughout the Bible. Solomon expressed this in his prayer of dedication of the Temple (1 Kings 8:41–43) where he prays for the foreigner who comes from a distant land because "they will hear of your great name and your mighty hand and your outstretched arm." The Psalms are replete with examples of the children of God praising his name for the purpose of reaching the nations.

Similarly, when Paul introduces the concept of sacrifice into the church he does so with mission in mind (Rom. 12:1–2).[124] Again the question arises, offering sacrifices for what purpose or on behalf of whom? I would again suggest sacrifices are to be made on behalf of those inside the church as well as those outside. Starting in Romans 12:3, Paul gives guidance in a variety of relationships. Our sacrifices should be motivated by love (Rom 12:3–21), they should be observable by governing authorities (Rom. 13:1–7), and so on.

If correct, this significantly impacts church culture. As sacrifice is practiced in many evangelical churches, it is seen as something an individual gives up to better focus their attention on God say, for example, during Lent. While this is quite appropriate, the church may be missing an incredible opportunity to develop a more redemptive culture. How would the church be different if we anchored the concept of sacrifice in its broader Old Testament context? What if we saw our sacrifices as giving up something costly on behalf of others rather than ourselves? I think this better fits the Old Testament culture in which both metaphors are developed as well as the argument of both Paul and Peter.

The combination of sacrifice and priesthood can be very powerful in today's world. Jobes has argued that when the church together acts as priests and brings the sacrifices that God desires forward, they are bringing the kingdom of God into the present world.[125] These two metaphors have a common element... they force us outside of ourselves. Most Christians think of these metaphors as related exclusively to our personal holiness, *rather than our mission*. While our personal holiness is quite important, I believe understanding these two metaphors in their original Old Testament context moves them beyond *personal holiness* to *missional behavior*. We are priests created to offer sacrifices that God desires on behalf of others. This is an essential aspect of creating a redemptive culture within a church in that we are motivated to move with love and sacrifice into the lives of each other and our cultures.

One more point. Rituals are an important part of church life. As argued above they serve several purposes including shaping a culture, expressing our theology in experiential ways, giving us common practices, and so on. As I have observed rituals in a variety of settings, I have noticed that rituals done well bring Christ into the present life of those practicing the rituals. Conversely, rituals done poorly often have the impact of shielding the person from the truth and, even worse, giving them a tradition that simply makes them feel good. Rituals done well, like theology, should bring Christ into our present lives in such a way that generates life and creates healthy community.

The Role of the Holy Spirit

This brings us to our final theological point. We discussed earlier that those who struggle with sin typically either enjoy freedom and joy or entrapment and struggle. Why the difference? Why don't they all struggle? This requires that we say a word about the Holy Spirit and how we work together with him in ministry.

As with the other areas of theology, this is a vast area of study. In order to grasp the interplay between the Spirit and the Christian let us start with a simple idea. There is no Christian who has the power to bring about conviction, redemption, or transformation in the life of another! This is uniquely and solely the responsibility of the Holy Spirit.

This fact alone should challenge many redemptive schemes found in the church today.

As argued earlier, the very heart of the New Covenant was the sending of the Spirit which would include creating a new heart and cleansing God's people. Jesus adds further information about the Spirit in John 16:8–15 that directly impacts our study. Here, the Spirit will "prove the world to be in the wrong" (John 16:8). As the various translations demonstrate, the word translated "prove" has a large range of meaning.[126] For our purposes, we will focus on the convicting aspect.

To begin, in John it is ultimately the world, rather than Jesus, who is on trial. This passage identifies the threefold responsibility of the Spirit using trial imagery.[127] Jesus portrayed the Spirit in terms of counselor and judge. Imagine for a moment, the situation in which the disciples found themselves. Jesus knew they were confused and nervous about his leaving. In this final conversation he encouraged them by identifying the role of the Spirit (John 16:8–11) and then affirmed that he would still be connected to them (John 16:12–15). The Spirit would act as a guide because he would receive his instruction from Jesus himself (John 16:14). In the coming months and years, this would become important as they had to navigate the challenges of their world. By extension, this is the very same situation pastors and leaders face today.

Jesus went further and explained the role of the Spirit using courtroom imagery. The first step was to identify the charge against the world—refusal to believe in Jesus (John 16:9). This fundamental charge goes back to the Garden when Adam and Eve rebelled against God (Gen. 3:5–7). This is the consistent pattern of all humanity (John 12:37–38, quoting Isa. 53:1). As discussed earlier, this was also Paul's argument in Romans 1:18–32. The basic sin of all people is to put oneself above God.

The second step was to identify the standard by which to hold the accused accountable—righteousness (John 16:10). The addition of Jesus' statement about going to the Father served as "God's confirmation of this standard in Jesus."[128] In other words, what appeared to be a victory of the world in the crucifixion of Jesus actually turned out to be proof of their rebellion and his righteousness.

Third, the final judgment was delivered—guilty (John 16:11). But it is more than the guilt of the world. We now see that behind the rebellion stands one greater. There is a bigger picture in every story of rebellion. This was the underlying motif in Judas' betrayal (John 13:27). Satan's influence helps us understand the deceitfulness of sin discussed earlier.

The question that arises is the rate at which the Spirit convicts. As Jesus continued, he brought encouragement to the disciples by letting them know they would not be left alone (John 16:12–15). Remember, the disciples would soon be in unknown territory after Christ left. Christ knew they could only handle so much (John 14:12). The role of the coming Spirit would be to guide them into all truth. What truth? Borchert, rightfully I believe, argues that this truth relates to all that the disciples would need after Jesus' resurrection. "The focus is upon one's life-defining orientation with God and in turn how that affects the way one is *guided* and related to the various information highways of life."[129]

This concept of guiding another is a critical aspect of creating a redemptive culture. The very story of the disciples powerfully illustrates this. As has been noted by many others, it is intriguing that the conversion of the disciples was not recorded for our benefit. What is clear is that by the end of the story, their faith had become real and they were living out that faith by the power of the Spirit. The Gospels are replete with stories and vignettes of the disciples learning, failing, making mistakes, learning again, making more mistakes, and so on. And through it all, Jesus demonstrated great patience as he led and guided them through the various challenges in their journey to maturity. If Jesus is the primary example, then we have a working model of what a redemptive culture should be like.

What we know from these stories is that it is the Holy Spirit who does the convicting, redeeming, and transforming. My experience reveals that his timetable is never the same as mine and it is different with each person. Our western culture, I believe, causes us to assume that because these ideas are captured in the form of imperatives, they must happen quickly. This has the tendency of dictating how we approach those struggling with sin. It is worth asking if our church cultures are confrontational, demanding, and impatient, or welcoming, safe, and redemptive.

Not to be misunderstood, it is vital that we engage people struggling with sin! The question is how, at what rate, and in what manner? As I engage people about their sin, I have seen people not yet ready for conviction, people who are convicted very quickly of sin, and people who take years before the reality of the destructiveness of their sin leads them to repentance. In each case, I have no authority or power to influence the rate that this occurs. It is solely and exclusively the responsibility of the Spirit.

The story of the disciples showed incredible patience by Jesus as he guided them to greater levels of maturity. I believe it is wiser to be patient and create multiple pathways of redemption. By this I mean that each person that enters the church needs a safe place to learn about Jesus. As they learn about Jesus, the more natural route is to transform at the rate that the Holy Spirit works in their life.

This leads me to my final point about the Spirit. Since he is on a different timetable than I am, it is critical that I am sensitive to that timetable when working with people struggling with sin. Sure, Matthew 18:15–17 lays out a process, but it does not necessarily capture a time element. Every pastor knows that some people listen and repent quickly while others are much slower. This is all part of developing a redemptive culture. Even the final step in the Matthew 18 passage is not clear. Keener argues that this step requires public disassociation.[130] Osborne similarly states Christ is talking about excommunication, but then is quick to suggest that the pastoral concern does not end with excommunication.[131] David Turner suggests this involves withdrawing community fellowship, but then notes that Jesus himself "treated notorious sinners compassionately."[132] What if something else is at work in this passage?

Given the model of Jesus' love for sinners I am inclined to believe that this final step is far more complex than excommunication. Yes, Keener is correct that the Jewish practices would have led to separation, but Jesus himself modeled and taught a very different response. There is no example of him "excommunicating" a pagan or tax collector. In fact, the story of Peter is illustrative here. He had heard Jesus teaching about not swearing by an oath (Matt. 5:33–37) and not publicly disowning him (Matt. 10:32–33), and yet he did these very things (Matt. 26:69–75).[133] In fact, if we take the Sermon on the Mount (Matt. 5–7) seriously, every believer lives with sin in some constant form since lust, hatred, and so on are more common than we admit.

The post-resurrection story is important here. We know that Jesus had predicted Peter's denials (Matt. 26:31–35) and that he had taught Peter the consequences of disowning and swearing by an oath. And yet, Jesus did not deny Peter before the Father (Matt. 10:33). Rather, he pursued Peter patiently for the purpose of restoring him (John 21:15–19).[134] At some level, Jesus' teachings represent the perfect standard, and yet, all pastors know that this is rarely a possibility. Most pastors live with the daily tension of the now—not yet reality of sin and redemption in a broken world. Jesus' examples provide a way through this in that most of time we have no better option than to choose the most redemptive path available to us.

Summary

Developing a redemptive culture within our churches is a complex, perhaps daunting task that requires much patience. Healthy cultures do not evolve naturally. They must be intentionally thought through, managed, and shaped. At the heart of a healthy culture are relationships. At the individual level, it is crucial that we help our people wrestle with sin and redemption in patient and loving ways. But this is not enough. As our people wrestle with their own lives, this must translate into the church culture at-large. But even this is not enough. It is crucial that the larger culture surrounding our churches look at us and see an attractive presentation of Christianity. In order for this type of authenticity to develop we must carefully consider how our interpretation and decisions impact church life and are received by church members.

First, the combination of understanding the actual nature of sin and the process of redemption allows us to make decisions that better engage our people and lead to a growing awareness in our local cultures of the health (or lack) of our churches. Sin is costly and must be addressed. Jesus' examples give us insight into how to address this. He was patient, yet willing to expose. He was gentle, yet willing to engage. He never shied away from entering people's lives but did it in very loving ways.

Second, as we develop redemptive church cultures we are, in effect, helping people understand that they have choices. They can continue in their sin which takes them deeper into mediocrity, often resulting in destruction in relationships, or they can choose the better path. But it is not in our purview to directly make this happen. This is uniquely the role of the Holy Spirit. All we can do is present the options and patiently walk with them at whatever rate the Holy Spirit moves them. In a later chapter we will discuss the unity of believers in the presence of sin and how to protect the church.

Third, as we learn to better act as priests and offer sacrifices on behalf of our people, we are simultaneously blessing them and modeling for the world what authentic Christian love looks like. In other words, we are acting as priests who are offering appropriate sacrifices. Churches do not need marketing plans beyond simply caring for and helping those struggling with loss, hurt, pain, grief, and so on. Our surrounding cultures are looking at us already! They are aware of our inconsistencies and hypocrisies. This provides us with unprecedented opportunities to make them aware of our loving patience to help people move to better places.

Finally, while we cannot, and should not attempt to, replace the role of the Spirit, we have the ability to interpret the Bible consistently along redemptive lines and ask how our decision-making enhances or detracts from this process. If our decisions detract from creating redemptive cultures, then we should check our interpretation.

Chapter 4

KEEPING THE LINE IN THE SAND

I recently sat on a panel of pastors in a seminary classroom addressing the current issue of sexual orientation. As each person presented their viewpoints it became clear to me that what was driving some of them was the earnest desire to attract unbelievers to their churches. I was reminded once again, that everyone has an overarching hermeneutic that drives their interpretations, and eventually their decisions. Many of their arguments tended to flow along one of two lines. Either take an inflexible approach and marginalize people, or compromise and welcome people. I would suggest that this polarized thinking is not biblical. How do we maintain integrity with Scripture and yet welcome people, no matter what they struggle with or how they live their lives?

Our third principle is that *our interpretation and decisions should be consistent with the freedoms established by the Bible itself.* As those who are versed in the debate on gender roles are aware, the parties on each side of the argument are convinced that their perspective is biblical and correct. It is important for us to remember that our broader culture is critical of Christianity and struggles to understand how God can be a loving God. I believe this is largely based on our approaches to current issues and how we address sin as discussed earlier.

Up to this point I have approached the challenge from a position of freedom. It is now time to clarify what we mean by freedom. To be clear, I do not mean unrestrained freedom. We cannot do whatever we desire. We are bound by the teachings of Scripture. But what does this mean?

Freedom

A good place to start in understanding Christian freedom is with Galatians 5:1, "It is for freedom that Christ has set us free. Stand firm, then, and do not let yourselves be burdened again by a yoke of slavery." This is the reason for Christ's work; that Christians may enjoy the liberation and freedom accomplished by the gospel.[135] When we discuss freedom, to what are we specifically referring?

The language of freedom and slavery is the central point of the allegorical comparison of Hagar and Sarah (Gal. 4:21–31). Hagar represents the slavery bound up with unbelief (Gal. 4:25). In contrast, Sarah represents the freedom one experiences through belief (Gal. 4:26). What Paul did was to "draw out the implications of the doctrine of justification by faith alone and to describe what it meant for the believer who had 'died to the law' now to 'live for God' (Gal. 2:19)."[136] But Paul drew out these implications, specifically in the language of freedom.

Similarly, he addressed this same concept in Romans 6. He opened Romans 6 by arguing that the believer has been baptized with Christ into his death with the result that the believer has died to sin in order to live a new life (Rom. 6:1–4). This dying to sin through baptism relates back to the death that resulted through our connection with Adam (Rom. 5:12–21). Because we died with Adam, sin reigns and we have no choice but to obey it. At the heart of his argument is an enslavement metaphor.

Slavery, as a theological metaphor, captures the tyrannical nature of being held in bondage. Even though slaves had rights, they were still *owned* by another and without freedom. This imagery was well-suited for Paul's argument to help us understand the nature of freedom. The enslavement metaphor would have been easily understood by Paul's audiences as "somewhere between one- and two-thirds of the population were either slaves or former slaves... this social reality is the basis of the comparison Paul draws with service to sin."[137] Only death with Christ frees people from such enslavement to sin. This slavery-freedom imagery, therefore, forms the basis for what it means to live freely as a Christian today.

This freedom that we have been granted is nuanced very carefully by Paul in Romans 6:12–23. Our freedom does not mean complete and full autonomy. Rather, we are now bound by our allegiance to Christ. As is true with all who have been set free from any restraining circumstances, freedom brings responsibility. This is why Paul can argue "you are slaves to the one you obey—whether you are slaves to sin, which leads to death, or to obedience, which leads to righteousness... You have been set free from sin and have become slaves to righteousness" (Rom. 6:17–18).

Most will recognize this in everyday life. Alcoholics trying to break free from the clutches of alcoholism are well-known for their belief that they are "recovering alcoholics." They recognize that they are always one step away from enslavement again. This is true for so many areas of sin in our society. In order for them to enjoy their freedom, it is necessary that they practice responsibility in all that they do. It is no wonder that this was a great metaphor for life in the Spirit.

Limitation

Since freedom is a central part of our study, we must also nuance this freedom. Remember, our thesis is that where the Bible is unclear in its direction, we have freedom and must learn to use that freedom well. Are there guidelines that we can follow to ensure the responsible use of our freedom?

Back to Galatians. Paul argues further, "You, my brothers and sisters, were called to be free. But do not use your freedom to indulge the flesh; rather serve one another humbly in love" (Gal. 5:13). Similar to Jesus, he then sums up the law with the quote from Leviticus 19:18 to "Love your neighbor as yourself" (Gal. 5:14). As discussed, and defined earlier, our life has been reframed by the requirement to love others. The remainder of Galatians is an explanation of what this means in the life of the church. Paul was well aware of the constant tension between balancing freedom with responsibility (Gal. 5:17).

It is important to note that freedom is a *calling*. As Timothy George argues, "you were called for a purpose—to be free!"[138] In other words, believers should now exercise their freedom appropriately *because* that is what they were created to do all along. As argued throughout the earlier chapters in this study, freedom with responsibility consistently appears in a variety of forms throughout Scripture. The freedom to choose was present right from the beginning in the Garden, and it has manifested itself throughout the history of the world, obviously including the freedom to sin.

It is also important to remember that this section in Galatians 5 is theologically essential in understanding Paul's argument. In other words, it is the theological outworking of his argument that "the *only* way one can live a godly life is by the Spirit, which does *not* come through returning to Torah."[139] It is freedom! But it is a freedom bound by love for others.[140] As Scot McKnight argues, "While 'love' is not the only 'fruit' of the Spirit, it is the most important to Paul (cf. vv. 6, 13–14; also Rom. 5:5; 1 Cor. 13; Col. 3:14). It summarizes the demand of God's law (Gal. 5:14)."[141]

Freedom and Limitation in Tension

I asked the question earlier of whether God intends that the Bible answer every question directly, or does he desire something else from his people. This Galatians passage surfaces the very real tension of living in freedom while living under the Spirit's guidance. It is not that Paul did not have rules and regulations available to him. He could have appealed to the law or to Jesus' teachings. By not doing so, he was "leaving these as *options*. He did not see the teachings of Jesus as new laws, nor would he appeal to the law of Moses as binding on the Christian. Instead, Paul described the essence of Christian living as 'freedom in the Spirit.'"[142]

This leaves open the very real possibility of moving in the direction of either legalism or licentiousness. This is where Christian maturity becomes essential. These are not in opposition to each other, but rather represent a common challenge: living under the guidance of the Spirit in Christian maturity and demonstrating responsible freedom while maintaining integrity with Scripture. This is the essence of this study.

Paul's approach in Galatians 5 is to navigate between these two extremes. He begins with the exhortation "do not let yourselves be burdened again by a yoke of slavery" (Gal. 5:1). In contrast, he urges "do not use your freedom to indulge the flesh" (Gal. 5:13). The way through is expressed in terms of love (Gal. 5:13–14). It is love that keeps the church from biting, devouring and destroying each other (Gal. 5:15). This is why he can conclude concerning the fruit of the Spirit, that "against such things there is no law" (Gal. 5:23).

The fulfillment of the law is *ultimately* the outcome of living according to the Spirit (Romans 8:4). Thus, the law eventually finds its fulfillment in the Christian life under the power of the Spirit. In other words, it is not through *compliance* that the law is fulfilled, but through the *action* of demonstrating genuine love for each other. And this, according to Paul, is what happens when we submit to the Spirit's leadership and guidance. As Christians, our task is that we must first convince ourselves that God's Spirit is the primary guide in our pursuit of God. "We must thoroughly grasp God's goodness in his granting to us the Holy Spirit as the sure guide to holiness and love."[143] Maturity is living by spiritual principles and not rules, all motivated by love of others.

The Role of Experience

How does this relate to interpretation and decision-making? How we utilize the Scriptures is vital in that it establishes more than acceptable behaviors. It establishes our created design and identifies how we were designed to live life. But it does this while simultaneously modeling how we engage those struggling with behaviors the Bible calls sin. In other words, we are talking about what type of culture we should be developing and how we are to make decisions that support that culture. This is why I am arguing that where the Bible is clear we should obey it and where the Bible is unclear, we have freedom... freedom to bless others and bring life to them.

It is easy to say this, but very challenging to practice in the daily life of a church. We are, in effect, talking about the tension between interpreting the Bible experientially and interpreting the Bible rationally. As one trained in hermeneutics, I find this tension to be present on a regular basis. While I exegete the Scriptures on a weekly basis as I was trained, I am also constantly working to bring the text into the lives of my church members and students such that they draw closer to the Lord and are more intrigued by his Word. Keener has argued that "it defeats the purpose of having a Bible if it simply becomes a mine for *what we hope to find there anyway.*"[144]

Let us be honest. We cannot come to the text without looking at it through the lens of our experience. We argued earlier that this dynamic was present in the Jerusalem Council (Acts 15). The Scriptures are meant to engage our people in their relationship with God in relevant and authentic ways as they experience life. This means that we should come to the Scriptures with the genuine hope that our lives can be different. This was Paul's argument in Romans 15:4, "For everything that was written in the past was written to teach us, so that through the endurance taught in the Scriptures and the encouragement they provide we might have hope." To simply read the Scriptures academically is improper and, worse, robs our people of hope.[145]

Coming to the Bible experientially is beneficial.[146] As a pastor, there have been numerous times when the psalms have provided comfort to one who is struggling. To sit with a person, when their life has now been reduced to days or weeks due to cancer, is an incredible honor. For an example from my own life, I lost my first wife when I was 25. I simply could not understand the pain and loneliness, and the daunting thought of raising my one and three-year-old children alone. My friends surrounded me and walked with me through this long, painful, and arduous journey. At their recommendation, I read and found comfort in Psalm 34:18 every day and often many times a day, "The Lord is close to the brokenhearted and saves those who are crushed in spirit."

As Keener has further argued, we are *invited* to approach the Scriptures experientially. "We can try to reconstruct [the psalms] historical situation…, or compare them with liturgical forms from surrounding cultures… But once we have done all possible research, psalms by their very genre invite us to do more than study them: they invite us to pray them, sing them, or use them as models to jumpstart our own prayers."[147] And, I would add, to bring us encouragement in times of deep suffering. The Scriptures summon believers "to feed on Jesus, the bread of life, to crave him as our very source of life."[148]

With our experience, we have now entered into the "art" part of Ramm's definition of hermeneutics. If we acknowledge both ideas that studying Scripture inductively remains the ideal (the science of hermeneutics), but experiential reading is inevitable (the art of hermeneutics), we are now beginning to grasp the bigger challenge of bringing the wisdom of the Scriptures into the church environment. This is no easy task.

As the apostles wrote in their letter to the Gentiles, "It seemed good to the Holy Spirit and to us" (Acts 15:28). Their decision was based on several factors. It included thoughtful reasoning as they worked through their theology. But it also included their experience and what they had learned from the Cornelius incident in Acts 10 and how God had previously acted. And even beyond this, it included discussion and debate between disparate parties with differing theological opinions. It is intriguing that prayer is not emphasized in this decision; they were expected, and *had confidence in the Holy Spirit*, that all of these factors would lead them to a wise conclusion.

And yet, to be sure, we must always remember that God gave us the Bible in its present form for a reason. As Craig Bartholomew reminds us, the Bible "comes into existence at a certain historical point: in all its synchronicity, it is embedded in history, and it is crucial that this historical aspect of the text be taken seriously in interpretation."[149] In other words, the Bible came to us *already contextualized*. This is why traditional hermeneutics is critical as we work to hear the Bible in its original context so that we can effectively bring forward the wisdom and teachings of the Bible.

If biblicism is guilty of blindly holding to the Bible as the only source of knowledge, we do not want to err in the opposite direction by allowing either our experience or our "hearing from the Spirit" to dominate our practices. I have tried to say this in various ways throughout this study. Effectively bringing the wisdom of the Scriptures into our church contexts requires listening carefully to the Spirit, inviting the community of the saints into the discussion, and measuring all decisions against the standard and stories of the Bible.

A Proposed Model

So, how do we bring our principles of hermeneutics along with our experiences and the voice and wisdom of the Holy Spirit together to make these sorts of wise decisions on a daily basis while still maintaining integrity with the Scriptures?

John Stackhouse has proposed a paradigm to work through this tension.[150] His foundational principle to start the discussion is that "The quest is not for the *perfect* theory, the *perfect* interpretation of Scripture, the *perfect* theology but for the best available. The main thing in life is not to figure everything out but to rely on God to provide what we need to accomplish his will in every circumstance—including the best theology for the job—and then to get on with the work."[151]

I agree. This is what I meant earlier when I argued that a more effective theological approach is to step back and ask a more basic question; namely, "What is our faithful response to be?" rather than, "What is the biblical thing to do?" In other words, is it possible to be "biblical" without being faithful to the redemptive nature and movement of God recorded in Scripture? Conversely, is it possible to be faithful, while deviating from a biblical imperative? I think both are possible.

After reviewing many of the passages related to gender, Stackhouse concludes that there is "an intriguing pattern of doubleness."[152] In other words, there are passages that do not fit well together, disagree in their application, contradict each other, and perhaps even create mutually exclusive situations.[153] My evangelical upbringing led me to always work to synthesize Scripture such that there were no contradictions. As I have studied the Scriptures over the years, I have come to similar conclusions as Stackhouse that there is not always a consistent and clear route to application. In fact, where doubleness occurs, this should cause us to rejoice because we are moving into the realm of freedom and the corresponding responsibility to exercise that freedom prudently.

This pattern of doubleness leads me to believe that this was intentional on God's part. The question is why? If the Bible was crystal clear at every point it would present numerous theological challenges. First, we would now have a rule book on our hands which would lead us toward Pharisaic practices (in the poorest sense of that word). Second, there would no longer be any need to work together in faith as the rules would be clear. Third, it would remove the very freedom (and creative expression) that we were created to experience and enjoy. Finally, it would short-circuit the process of working toward unity and leave us with only the option of unanimity.

Regarding this last point, one of the great joys of pastoring a church with many denominations present and with varying theological positions is the challenge and result of successfully setting aside our differences and "striving together as one for the faith of the gospel" (Phil. 1:27). Our very by-laws state, "As a non-denominational community church that serves people from a wide variety of Christian traditions, we embrace the following famous statement from Augustine, Erasmus and many Christian bodies since then and seek to have: In essentials–Unity, In non-essentials–Freedom, In all things–Charity." This distinction assumes that there are differences, or doubleness, to be worked through in the Scriptures.

The way we manage this in our context is to all agree on the essentials, but enjoy the freedoms of discussion and debate on non-essentials.[154] With so many variations in theological positions we have to work diligently to debate and discuss well, all the while staying focused on mission and maintaining unity. While this is challenging, the fruit of this work creates a very engaging, life-giving, and healthy environment.

Therefore, I am proposing that Stackhouse's observation on doubleness is not only accurate, but theologically essential for a well-developed ecclesiology and mission focus. Not only does it lead to great dependence on each other, it also provides a model for the world of what genuine community looks like as we work to overcome our different theologies. I would suggest that the world does not want a church that "has it all figured out." I know I do not. The mystery is what draws most people into a deeper walk.

Examples

Stackhouse's model assumes that, just as there is a pattern of doubleness in Scripture, there are also points wherein the Scriptures are clear and provide certain direction. My proposal, therefore, is where the Bible is clear—has drawn a line in the sand—we should obey it without reservation. Conversely, where there is doubleness, we have freedom to explore possible options. Does this freedom mean we can do whatever we like? Absolutely not! The whole purpose of this study is to identify the other principles, or questions that need to be asked, that clarify and limit that freedom within boundaries. These other principles establish our range of interpretation.

With this in mind, I propose the following possible examples of both doubleness and certainty. I recognize that not everyone will agree with these examples. I simply ask that you capture the idea of the proposal and work within your own theological tradition to "make the best decision one can make about what Scripture means; and then to respond to it in faith, obedience, and gratitude."[155]

This raises one more question worth considering. Are we afraid of getting our interpretation wrong? Or more precisely, are we going to make mistakes? In my church context with varying theological traditions, this is a question that we address regularly. In my own life, I have learned that my theology has developed in vast areas as I have moved from a new believer through seminary education to educator and then to holding a senior pastor position. Somewhere along the way I became comfortable with the fact that my theology will never be perfect. I am grateful for a gracious God who has guided me skillfully along the way to better theology and application. I think this is one of the key lessons to be taken from the story of Jesus' encounter with the Samaritan woman in John 4. It is better to be faithful than correct!

So, with this in mind I offer the following examples.[156]

Examples of Patterns of Doubleness.[157]

Divorce (Matt. 5:31–32). While it was originally allowed for the husband to issue a certificate for divorce (Deut. 24:1–4), Jesus condemned what was once allowed. "As the definitive eschatological teacher of the law, his interpretation was based on the original divine intent for marriage, not the expediency of the moment. The Pharisees' overly permissive interpretation capitalized on a concession to human sinfulness."[158]

It is well-known that there were various schools of thought within the Jewish leadership regarding divorce. Here, Jesus showed us more deeply "how relationships are to function in the kingdom age by addressing the deepest relationship of all, marriage."[159] He went beyond the Jewish leadership by making marriage lifelong and restricting divorce. Is Jesus' teaching the final answer? Possibly not, as Paul named other exceptions. For example, he permitted divorce when an unbelieving spouse ends the marriage (1 Cor. 7:15–16). This was not discussed by Jesus. Paul, in the Corinthian Epistles, dealt with a divided church and navigated the associated challenges in order to bring unity back into the fellowship. In this regard, he followed the example of Christ in that he established priorities to help guide the church in the restoration of unity.

Every pastor has to make these kinds of decisions daily. For example, a wife makes the decision to divorce her husband because of inappropriate sexual activity with their children. Which is the greater of the sins, or which is the lesser of the two evils? I would suggest the best redemptive approach is to ask which choice is the spiritually healthiest of all the presenting options.

Gender roles.[160] At one level, Jesus repeatedly "trespasses across the gender lines of his culture to affirm, serve, and enjoy women as he also delights in them." As the Holy Spirit was poured out at Pentecost, men and women together were the recipients (Acts 2:16–18). Paul declared that in Christ all the barriers that separate people from one another are removed, including the gender barrier (Gal. 3:28). Spiritual gifts were distributed equally without regard to their gender (Rom. 12:6–8; 1 Cor. 12:8–10, 27–30; Eph. 4:11).

And yet, the consistent pattern in the Bible is one of patriarchy: men were in charge. Jesus welcomed women into this group of disciples, but not his inner circle. Similarly, Paul, in spite of the debates, seemed to place some restraints on women in different contexts. Women apparently were to keep silent, and yet were permitted to speak at other times (1 Cor. 11:5; 14:33–35). There were some limitations placed on their teaching (1 Tim. 2:11–12). I am aware of the complexities surrounding these arguments. My intent is not to solve these debates but to illustrate Stackhouse's argument.

Regarding women's silence, Stackhouse argues that "Paul believes that women should keep silent in church *and* that they should pray and prophecy. How can they do both?" He argues further,

> Paul is guided by the Holy Spirit—even used by the Holy Spirit without his full awareness of the implications—to do two things simultaneously: (1) to give the church prudent instructions as to how to survive and thrive in a patriarchal culture that he thinks will not last long; and (2) to maintain and promote the egalitarian dynamic already at work in the career of Jesus that in due course will leave gender lines behind. This doubleness in Paul—which we can see also in the ministry of Jesus—helps to explain why egalitarians and complementarians both find support for their views in Paul's writings. It is this doubleness that is the key to this paradigm on gender.[161]

Eating meat offered to idols. "In some cases, what is troubling to some is declared to be of no consequence, *unless* such a thing would trouble one's conscience or cause another Christian confusedly to stumble back into sinful ways."[162] This is part of the challenge for the interpreter in working through 1 Corinthians 8, 10:25–30, and Romans 14:14–23.

Women in leadership. Stackhouse raises another example of doubleness when he points toward current practices. "There are not simply two positions on gender among evangelicals but several. For example, some evangelicals allow women to preach but only in foreign missionary situations. Others allow women to participate in spiritual leadership but only in so-called parachurch organizations, not in congregations or denominations. Still others permit women to have wide-ranging theological careers of speaking and writing as long as they profess to be responsible to a man, whether husband or pastor or both."[163]

Cultural shifts. Although not necessarily an example of doubleness in the Bible, Stackhouse asks the question, "What are Christians supposed to do when society itself shifts to egalitarianism?"[164] He is correct that there is now no longer a rationale within culture itself for women to remain in culturally expected roles of dependence and submission. What is the church to do in this situation? He raises the possibility that Christians are lagging behind society in that it is common in certain traditions to require a submissive role for women.

Examples of certainty.

Trinity. As an evangelical I hold unswervingly to trinitarianism. It is the foundation for all that I believe and for the outworking of all theology in the life of the church. I personally see no doubleness in this core doctrine of the church. Stanley Grenz has well stated that "the concept of tri-unity lies at the heart of the unique biblical understanding of God, and therefore Christians through the years have seen it as crucial for maintaining the central message of the Bible."[165]

Adultery. Jesus' teaching in the Sermon on the Mount (Matt. 5:27–30) preserves the fundamental Old Testament teaching that adultery is sin. He expanded the concept of what constitutes adultery in his teachings, and, while making allowances, at no point did he claim it as acceptable behavior. The controversy comes more in the area of how to respond. Perhaps this study will give some guidance.

Homosexuality. In spite of the current debate, I see no deviation from the biblical teaching that homosexuality is sinful. Without getting into the debate, the Bible never waivers, and shows no pattern of acceptance.[166] And yet, while I do not see doubleness regarding the biblical teachings on sexual orientation, I do see variation developing on how to respond and engage the debate. As with adultery, perhaps this book will give some guidance.

Summary

These few examples are enough to illustrate Stackhouse's proposal. As Stackhouse suggests, let us face the reality of studying the Bible. It is complex and arouses a variety of responses among Christians who also have varying experiences. Additionally, as every pastor knows, there are many situations wherein the Bible is either unclear, or where no immediate option is available which satisfies God's desired outcome.

I agree with Stackhouse's conclusion that these tensions reveal that some things matter more than others. "God is willing to forgo the achievement of secondary objectives in the interest of furthering his primary purposes, and he expects us to do the same."[167] I believe that Paul is not trying to develop a theology of gender nor create a blueprint for Christian conduct, except to show us how to navigate these complex areas when contrasting the biblical history and teachings, the surrounding culture, and God's ultimate plan for his creation. Using the principles of accommodation, we can see that God works within the constraints of human limitation to redeem the world according to his plan. As we discussed earlier, he pursues shalom in spite of the mess we have made. More on this in the next chapter.

Thus, I suggest that where the Bible draws a line in the sand, we should leave the line where it is drawn. Conversely, when the Bible makes allowances or creates doubleness, we have freedom. Again, freedom to do whatever? Absolutely not. We must at this point go back to Principles #1 and #2.

If we go down the road of normalizing sin, then we create additional theological challenges that limit our ability to fulfill God's mission. First, we have removed the need for redemption. Remember our earlier discussion of sin. The identification of sin is not for the purpose of judgement, shame, or control. Rather it is for the purpose of redemption. In each case of sin, would the person be happier if they experienced redemption in that area of life, no matter how long it took? I believe so.

Second, if we are not careful, we model for the world that morality does not matter. This is the opposite problem of creating judgmental and critical church cultures. If morality does not matter, why go to church? We become nothing more than a social club, and there are plenty of those to go around.

Third, we risk sending the underlying message that the Bible does not matter and is not relevant. Many pastors deal with this question regularly in today's world. It is critical that we leave the lines where they are drawn but be willing to step across the lines into the messiness of whatever is on the other side. Our younger generations need to see integrity with the way we handle Scripture and redemptive challenges and provide life-giving answers when asked why we believe what we believe. It no longer works to say, "Because the Bible says so."

This raises one more point. Should we use the most conservative passage? At one level this makes sense. For example, my reading of 1 Corinthians 11 when compared to 1 Corinthians 14 demonstrates doubleness in gender roles, especially when compared to 1 Timothy 2. Why not take the more conservative position? If we think through the consequences of that approach, we find ourselves in deeper trouble than if we learn to discuss and demonstrate responsible freedom. What do we do with the slavery texts? The wearing of jewelry and braiding of the hair texts? If we take the most "conservative" passage, we are likely to find ourselves going backward from where we presently stand. The Bible is designed to enter into our lives wherever we are in history and to guide us to develop better redemptive approaches. I will discuss this in more detail in the next chapter.

What all this means is that our interpretations and decisions should be consistent with the freedoms established by the Bible. It is of no redemptive help to either create unwelcome environments or normalize sin. Where the Bible is consistent, so should we be. Conversely, where the Bible creates "doubleness," we should carefully work to create healthier and better redemptive approaches within our own cultural context. If our practices, rituals, traditions, and behaviors as a church do not lead to this result, we should check our interpretation.

Chapter 5

FOLLOWING THE
MOVEMENT OF GOD IN
BIBLICAL HISTORY

Once, when teaching in India, I raised the question of God's redemptive nature by using Deuteronomy 22:28–29 and the question of rape in the Bible. To challenge the students, I asked whether this verse represented the redemptive God we have come to know through the cross. If so, why don't we obey it today and if not, what is it doing as a command in the law? While my intent was to engage them in the discussion of how God redeems culture, they went in a different direction. The entire class was confused and so I asked, "If a woman is raped in your culture, would you expect her to marry the man who raped her?" In a stunned reply, the students (both male and female) responded with, "Who else is going to marry her?" I realized that, in this particular region, I had stepped across a great cultural divide. While this passage was not *directly* redemptive to me, it was clear that, in this particular cultural region, the guidance in this passage had redemptive value for these students in that the rape passages were meant to protect the victim and ultimately lead Israel in a new direction unknown in the ancient world.

Our fourth principle is that *our interpretation and decisions should be consistent with the theological development of the Bible as it unfolds.* This is asking a slightly different question than the third principle. As N. T. Wright, William Webb, Christopher J. H. Wright and others have shown, the Bible demonstrates consistent movement as God speaks into and interacts with his people. As such, applications and commands also demonstrate movement and possible trends related to areas of social, cultural, and personal concerns. This principle examines this movement and works to identify what is stable as well as what is relative to ensure that decisions regarding application are consistent with this movement of God and do not regress.

At one level, this is an easy principle. Who wants to go back to slavery? Who wants to implement greater controls over jewelry, head coverings, and so on? As we move beyond some of these obvious applications into challenges raised by culture, working through this principle involves some work, and often some level of complexity and deeper study. Who wants to limit women in leadership? Who wants to tackle the plethora of sins found in any congregation? Should we differentiate within our congregation between greed, murder, strife, malice, disobeying parents, and so on? (Rom. 1:28–32). How should we approach these various sins and on what basis? Understanding this principle lays a foundation for approaching these challenging questions.

The Questions of our World

I spend approximately 20 hours each week in restaurants, coffee shops, and bars talking to people about life. They are from all walks of life, different countries, different generations, different faith backgrounds, some with no faith backgrounds, and so on. The questions I routinely get about Christianity are fairly consistent. They are oriented toward making sense of the surrounding world. Often, a past Christian experience comes into the discussion in very powerful and dynamic ways. For the majority of these people, their church experience has led them *away* from the church. I believe this phenomenon is widely known today. Thus, there are a plethora of books working to address these questions.[168]

The questions cover a large expanse including the problem of evil, the reliability of the Scriptures, the relevance of the Bible and the church today, the authority of Scripture, the controlling nature of the church, religious pluralism, and so on. It is clear that today's generations are struggling with many facets of life and faith. It is apparent to me that today's church must reevaluate its relationship with culture and redesign its approaches to answer the more pressing cultural questions with better *biblical* and *theological* approaches.

My experience has led me to conclude that one of the core problems we face today is an inadequate way of interpreting *and applying* the Scriptures in our own cultural contexts. As discussed earlier, excellent interpretation does not always lend itself to effective application. I would suggest that proper interpretation and application *cannot* ultimately occur without the discussion being immersed in the ancient cultural context as well as addressing our present cultural contexts. Interpretation and application are in a symbiotic relationship with one another in that they depend on each other to challenge and inform the process.

This leads to the strength as well as weakness of higher education in that, while the classroom provides a sort of laboratory, it is also often removed from actual experience. This is not a criticism. I am deeply grateful for my seminary experience and the training I received in interpretation. However, moving into pastoral ministry surfaced a plethora of challenges not treated in the classroom and forced me to ask different questions of the text beyond its meaning.

I believe that to begin to answer this gap, we must go back again to some larger questions of the Bible and address more core issues in the story of God's redemptive movement within history. This approach is now being addressed in larger and more complex ways than ever before.[169] It is not my intention to move these discussions further, except to argue

that considering these current approaches is necessary if we are to elucidate Scripture to these younger generations in compelling ways, and
if we are to develop better redemptive approaches that are life-giving.

Renewing the Center[170]

When Grenz wrote *Renewing the Center*, he questioned whether
evangelical theology would be able to move forward in the "wake of
the demise of foundationalism."[171] The basic problem, as he saw it, was
that there were a number of growing voices that argued that the concept
of "basic beliefs" was no longer tenable. This is captured in the idea of
postmodern philosophy which is highly relative in orientation. It is not
my intent to engage this complex argument, except to note that Grenz
proposed basic beliefs that were, in fact, tenable and should guide our
development of theology. One of those basic beliefs relates to theological reflection within the context of community, rather than leaving it
in the purview of higher education.[172]

He notes that evangelicals are storytellers and that we naturally
understand our experiences in categories drawn from that experience,
as well as the narrative and teaching sections of Scripture (if we are
coming from a Christian background). "As evangelicals, therefore, we
have come to see the story of God's action in Christ as the paradigm of
our stories."[173] But what is that paradigm? I would suggest that the actual
paradigm utilized by most Christians to shape their decision-making has
more to do with their experience in life and their tradition, rather than
their theology (more on this later).

Grenz goes further and concludes that "experiences are always fil-
tered by an interpretive framework that facilitates their occurrence."[174]
In other words, for Christians and those with a Christian background,
understanding and interpretation of the world is dependent on what we
were taught. If we come from a judgmental background, we naturally
interact with that particular dynamic as we work to make sense of the

world around us. Similarly, if we come from a guilt-induced background, we struggle more with guilt, and so on.

With the younger generations, I believe the church has failed to adequately define both sin and redemption, especially as it relates to our freedom. In my experience, few are asking *what* the Bible says. Rather, if they are still curious, they are asking *why* the Bible says what it says. These are very different questions and require different approaches to developing answers that equip and give life. Grenz is moving in this direction when he states, "The theologian seeks to articulate what *ought* to be the interpretive framework of the Christian community."[175] In other words, theology should make sense of our surrounding world. For many in our world today, it does not! Perhaps we have failed to focus on some of the more major characteristics of God and his Word.

The Proposed Center of Evangelical Theology

How we develop theology *directly* impacts the culture of our churches. We may have values and theological statements hanging on the wall, but that does not mean those values and statements impact and create the culture envisioned in Scripture. The corporate world is replete with examples wherein the stated corporate values are misaligned with the actual operating values. One of the primary responsibilities of church leadership is to ensure integrity between *stated* values and beliefs and *actual* values and beliefs present in the congregation.

For example, in an earlier church I attended, I was asked by the leadership to assess the actual or working values of the congregation to see if they matched our stated values. I formed groups to assess this and took them through a series of exercises. By God's grace, there was a high degree of consistency in many areas. However, there was a glaring inconsistency when it came to the ability of our church to openly discuss areas of conflict. The study bore out that we were actually a conflict-avoidance church. In contrast to the senior pastor's belief and the stated value of open and genuine dialogue, most of the congregation felt that areas of conflict could not be openly discussed with the pastor! He was astounded.

His stated value did not match his actual lack of openness to discuss areas of conflict. My experience has convinced me that this is a very common problem in our churches today. It is extremely difficult work to develop theology that actually changes congregational behavior. This is why I argue that *how* we develop theology directly impacts our church cultures.

Arland Hultgren approaches this issue in a different manner when he states, "We must come to terms with the stark fact that many modern people do not share with the ancients a sense of their need for redemption at all. The world is not considered a place from which one needs to be rescued."[176] At one level, he is correct. The way the church has expressed the theology of redemption has often left church-goers uninterested or simply confused. By limiting the theology of redemption to Christ and his work for us as *individuals*, many people no longer see a need. What happens if this rich concept is broadened to include whole communities and even creation?

Grenz moves toward this when he states,

> Christian theology is the study of the narrative of this God fulfilling the divine purposes as disclosed in the Bible. The biblical narrative presents as the ultimate goal of the biblical God the establishment of community. Taken as a whole the Bible asserts that God's program is directed to the establishment of community in the highest sense of the word: a redeemed people, living within a redeemed creation, enjoying the presence of the triune God. Theology, in turn, is the explication of this divine goal.[177]

In other words, a central goal of our lived-out theology should be authentic community. Salvation is much more than the giving of eternal life (John 10:10). "At the heart of the Christian message is the declaration that the goal of life is community: fellowship with God, with others, with creation, and in this manner with oneself."[178] But, how do we get there? I would suggest that the journey starts with a healthier view of redemption, both in what is being accomplished as well as how the Bible reveals this central characteristic of God.

The Bigger Picture of Redemption

Earlier we discussed redemption and how it impacts relationships within the church. In this chapter I broaden the concept and look at how God is redemptive as expressed through the history recorded in the Bible. How we engage and elucidate the Scriptures to our people should be a key element in teaching a sound decision-making process while simultaneously developing a greater love for the Bible.

The words for redemption used in both the Old Testament and New Testament show a high degree of overlap. At one level, adequate work has been done to reveal how redemption impacts the individual. Most Christians are familiar at a basic level with the idea of redemption and forgiveness. However, I would suggest that the entire Bible is an example of redemption at a level rarely thought of by Christians.

The beginning of this journey is to understand redemption in this larger context before we look at more detailed stories in the Bible. As discussed earlier, the story of Ruth and Boaz exemplified well the concept of redemption within families and tribes. But isn't God bigger than this? "OT texts of various genres portray Yahweh as the divine *gōʾēl* who, like his familial counterpart, helps those who have fallen into need."[179]

The obvious example of this is the story of the exodus. This is the sense in which this word is used in Exodus 6:6, "Therefore, say to the Israelites: 'I am the LORD, and I will bring you out from under the yoke of the Egyptians. I will free you from being slaves to them, and

I will redeem you with an outstretched arm and with mighty acts of judgment.'" As discussed earlier, here he rescues a people who are unable to rescue themselves. This story is the key example of what Christ will accomplish for the entire world.

This is the background for several significant New Testament passages. For example, Zechariah can cry out with joy, "Praise be to the Lord, the God of Israel, because he has come to his people and redeemed them" (Luke 1:68). Similarly, Anna "gave thanks to God and spoke about the child to all who were looking forward to the redemption of Jerusalem" (Luke 2:38). While the word group related to redemption here envisages the promised restoration of Israel, it certainly has a bigger picture in view.[180] This is portrayed vividly in Christ's statement, "For even the Son of Man did not come to be served, but to serve, and to give his life as a ransom for many" (Mark 10:45). While greatly debated, it seems clear that Jesus has surrendered his life for many to bring about their rescue.

The purpose for raising these passages is to demonstrate that redemption covers a vast terrain. Richter and many others have appropriately linked the exodus and crucifixion events. In the Matthew account of the last supper, Jesus made the incredible claim, "Then he took a cup, and when he had given thanks, he gave it to them, saying, 'Drink from it, all of you. This is my blood of the covenant, which is poured out for many for the forgiveness of sins'" (Matt. 26:27–28). Since they were celebrating Passover, the exodus event was front and center on their minds. It was a very small step to connect Jesus' statement to Moses' statement at the ratification of the Sinai Covenant when he said, "Moses then took the blood, sprinkled it on the people and said, 'This is the blood of the covenant that the LORD has made with you in accordance with all these words'" (Exod. 24:8). "By means of oath and sacrifice, another rabble of slaves was about to be transformed into God's covenant-people."[181] This is redemption.

The Dignity and Destiny of Humanity

As we develop a more specific model for looking at the movement of God throughout history it is necessary to first ask the question, "What is God up to and why does he engage culture the way he does?" One of the clear dynamics taught in Scripture and experienced in life is that we have not yet reached the ultimate in human perfection and experience of joy. Every human carries some degree of hope that there is something better! This is actually captured by Paul when he claims "being confident of this, that he who began a good work in you will carry it on to completion until the day of Christ Jesus" (Phil. 1:6).

Paul, and the other authors of Scripture, place our lives in the midst of a long and protracted journey. But what is this journey and for what purpose? Additionally, how does this impact the way we interpret Scripture and make decisions. I would suggest understanding these questions is very helpful in developing a redemptive model to be used in churches.

Philip Hughes helps us begin this journey when he states, "man as created was not what he finally would be." He goes on to clarify that "[humanity's] destiny was to advance from glory to glory, and that, even if there had been no fall, the end was designed to be even more splendid than the beginning."[182] This is partly what is behind Paul's astonishing statement that he was to present "the word of God in its fullness" (Col. 1:25). He was carrying to completion his divine commission given to him by God. "The hope of completing this grand assignment within the space of a few decades was a tribute to the splendid *vision* which made the church of Christ in those days a fellowship of such vitality and power."[183] This is why Hughes, appropriately I believe, conceives of history in terms of destiny when he states, "What God started in creation he not only started in the Son, who is the Image after whom man is formed, but he also completed in the Son, who is the Image to whom all the redeemed are being conformed (Rom. 8:29; 2 Cor. 3:18)."[184]

If history is conceived of as destiny or a journey, this helps explain many of the complex stories in the Bible. At the heart of this journey is the concept of humanity being made in the image of God. John Kilner helpfully clarifies image as involving a special connection with God that results in our reflection to the rest of the world of the one true living God.[185] Marc Cortez explains further, "Paul portrays the image as something that is being 'transformed' (2 Cor. 3.18) and 'renewed' (Col. 3.10) in human persons as they are drawn ever close to the person of Christ."[186]

This concept lies at the heart of what it means for humans to have dignity. The dignity of humanity lies in being made in God's image and being able to reflect his glory to the rest of creation. It is not captured in human capacities such as the ability to reason, or human virtues such as righteousness, or the ability to rule over creation, and so on even though these are important distinctions. Because humans have dignity, they are worthy of value and respect, specifically because they are made in God's image! When viewed this way, the image of God and resulting dignity becomes "a 'hermeneutical lens' through which the reader is better able to understand the significance of what happens in history and where God's people are headed."[187]

This lays the foundation for understanding the larger story of the Bible. At its core, the story of the Bible is the story of redemption. This means that the various stories of the Bible capture the tension between kingdom values and cultural values. I would suggest that each New Testament Epistle, at some level, records the fine line each local church was walking between the cultural values in their locale, and the freedoms and kingdom values established by the New Covenant.

Because of the fallenness of humanity, our clear tendency is to go off track and move away from God (Rom. 1:18–32). And yet, we know that God values all of creation, *including culture*. So, how is being made in the image of God a hermeneutical lens that explains what God is doing?

Redemption as a Model of Hermeneutics

To answer this question, we must start with a very simple hermeneutical principle. *Whenever God acts or speaks into our culture he does
so for the purpose of redemption.* In other words, where we have moved
away from him and developed cultural values that are not consistent
with his desired will for humanity, he involves himself with us for the
specific purpose of restoring his original intent that we reflect his glory
and experience increasing levels of joy in our relationship with him.

This potentially leads to a different way of reading and interpreting
Scripture. Whatever text we are in, I believe we can start with some
basic assumptions. First, God is interested in redeeming what is wrong
with the ancient cultures in which the Bible is written. Second, he is
interested in reintroducing human dignity as part of his redemptive
involvement. Third, he is reframing culture, or starting a trajectory
that develops an ethic that is in keeping with his original design. In
other words, with each action and spoken word, he is "starting the ball
rolling" which finds its final reality in the Person of Christ. Ultimately,
this is captured in the Person of Christ as he is the human *par excellence* to which the church is being shaped and to which every human
should aspire.

Another way of saying this is that God consistently compromises
in his involvement with his creation for the sake of the gospel.[188] At
no point does he *desire* rape, and yet he allowed it to exist and even
regulated it for a period of time until he redeemed this broken area of
humanity. Similarly, he never desired genocide and yet he allowed it to
exist, until he brought about redemption in the way we relate to our
enemies. Even Jesus, when asked, replied to "give back to Caesar what
is Caesar's" (Matt. 22:21). This represents some level of compromise
as God surely did not desire all of the evil state-funded practices of the
Roman Empire.

As we move into the challenging and complex stories of the Old
Testament, these principles help us make sense of how God interacts

with the cultures of the world. These principles lie behind William Webb's redemptive-movement hermeneutic.[189] As he argues from the beginning, "It is necessary for Christians to challenge their culture where it departs from kingdom values; it is equally necessary for them to identify with their culture on all other matters."[190] I will not restate Webb's argument here, except to provide an example to illustrate how it can help us in our decision-making.

In Deuteronomy 25:1–3, the Israelites were given instructions for resolving disputes between parties. The people were to take their disputes to the court and the judges would decide the case. The judges were responsible for acquitting the innocent and condemning the guilty. If the person was found to be guilty, the judge was to make them lie down and have them "flogged" according to the crime committed. But the judge was limited to forty lashes, otherwise, the punishment would be considered degrading.

If we obeyed this passage today, we would appropriately be charged with some degree of assault or abuse. By all ethical standards today, this passage represents an unacceptable level of brutality. This immediately raises the question of the redemptive nature of God. If this represents the redemptive God that we know and worship today, why don't we obey this passage? If not, what is it doing as a command in the law?

The answer lies in understanding the redemptive nature of God within the context of the brutal nature of the surrounding cultures. The period of ancient Egypt that overlaps with the exodus of Israel provides an example.[191] A sampling of the Egyptian court rulings during this period reveals that beatings typically ranged from one hundred to two hundred blows, with five open wounds allowed in certain cases. When compared to the Egyptian discipline court limits, it becomes much easier to see how the forty-lash limit in Deuteronomy is a move in a redemptive direction. "No other ancient Near Eastern source limits the number of strokes.[192] My first hermeneutical assumption above is demonstrated in that God was interested in redeeming what was wrong with the ancient cultures in which the Bible was written.

My second assumption that he was interested in introducing human dignity as part of his redemptive involvement is born out in the Deuteronomy text itself. Deuteronomy 25:3 identifies the reason for the limitation; namely, degradation of a fellow Israelite would have occurred otherwise. Here, human dignity is presented as the reason for the limitation. "The concern for human dignity and the protection of the vulnerable continues in this law regarding corporal punishment."[193] J. G. McConville agrees, "It is significant that the explicit intention of the law is not to prevent the death of the offender (though that effect follows), but rather to preserve his dignity."[194]

My third hermeneutical assumption that God was reframing culture and starting a journey that developed an ethic that was in keeping with his original design ultimately found its reality in the Person of Christ and the later teachings of the New Testament. Jesus himself taught that we should turn the other cheek (Matt. 5:39), give more to those who sue us than what they ask (Matt. 5:40), go the extra distance for those who ask (Matt. 5:41), and love our enemies (Matt. 5:44).

Regarding Jesus' teaching, Turner reminds us that Jesus "reveals the ultimate meaning of the law of God for those whose righteousness must exceed that of the legal experts and the Pharisees."[195] Blomberg further argues that these teachings form the manifesto of the new community and therefore, the church "must try to permeate society with these ideals, albeit in a persuasive rather than coercive fashion."[196] The ethic taught by Jesus had clearly been developed further from the ancient teaching of Deuteronomy.

Paul goes further when he encourages us to bless those who persecute us (Rom. 12:14) and not to take revenge (Rom. 12:19). These admonitions take us further down this redemptive journey as he had to navigate cultural challenges and teach how to implement this developing ethic. The cultural situation of Romans occurred after the deportation of Jews and Jewish Christians under Emperor Claudius and subsequent return beginning at his death. This included those in the church who had not been deported as well as those who had.[197] In other words, the church was comprised of both Jews and Gentiles and thus presented cultural challenges in that this church had to navigate reestablishing unity in that some had been forced to leave and were now permitted back, while others were never asked to leave in the first place.

Into this cultural context, Paul introduced one of the core teachings of Jesus—genuine love for others (Romans 12:9). While evil is to be abhorred, Paul called for a humble and peaceable attitude toward others, both fellow Christians (vv. 10, 13, 16) and non-Christians (vv. 14, 17–21). If indeed, Paul was addressing some of the conflict resulting from the returning Jewish Christians, the contrast between Romans 12:13–14 (those in need and those who persecute) provide us with an excellent example of how this developing ethic was worked out within culture.[198] Roman values aside, we can see how, what was started in Deuteronomy 25, had a reframing impact in culture over time, so that by the time of Paul the original ethic had been significantly developed and revamped. I believe this was God's intention all along.

Summary

If we see the Bible as a record of God's incredible and loving redemptive engagement with culture for the purpose of restoration, then we can navigate how to interact with other cultures (including our own). Mission classes have long presented case studies in which students wrestle with the values of other cultures. For example, polygamy in other parts of the world. Is the answer simply to bring them up to the current ethic taught in Scripture, or to gently and patiently move them to a better ethic in a slow and redeeming fashion?

Back to the situation in India. I would suggest a simple model. Wherever we find an ethic that is lagging behind Scripture, we follow the pattern of God's graceful and patient engagement. In the case of the region of India I mentioned at the beginning of this chapter, perhaps the passages that moderate rape and begin to demonstrate redemptive movement toward healthier sexual ethics still apply.

In contrast, where cultural redemption has occurred, leave the biblical passages in the "museum of redemption" rather than attempt to enculturate them into today's developed system of ethics. It never fails to amaze me how many Christians attempt to turn slavery texts into human resource texts! Leave them as slavery texts and marvel at how God worked in despicable situations to bring about fresh and life-giving ways of relating to him and each other. If we believe that he is in the business of redeeming his own creation, then two things immediately are apparent. First, he has been redeeming culture all along. Second, he is still redeeming culture. It is preposterous to believe that he is finished!

A further note. While there is much discussion about absolute versus relative truth and the impact of postmodern philosophy, I believe that both are present in Scripture. As discussed earlier in leaving the line in the sand, all that the Bible teaches about God and the character of God is absolutely true. It may be an emerging theology in that God reveals himself slowly over time, but all that is true of God remains true of God and has always been true of God.

Conversely, in the areas of social and personal concerns, I believe the Bible shows consistent development. This should not be surprising as this seems to be God's preferred way of engaging his people. A simple illustration will suffice. I am much different now than I was many years ago when I turned to Christ in faith. That transition and growth did not happen *quickly*! But it did happen *steadily* as God revealed himself to me over time. As I learned more about him, I have become more loving, generous, patient, affectionate, and so on. Why would it be any different on a global scale with people groups?

As Webb has appropriately argued, "God in a pastoral sense accommodates himself to meeting people and society where they are in their existing social ethic and (from there) he gently moves them with incremental steps toward something better. Moving large, complex and embedded social structures along an ethical continuum is by no means a simple matter."[199] I would add that moving individual people along an ethical continuum is also no simple matter.

This is the very story of Israel. The history of Israel is the story of God's redemptive and loving engagement with them to produce for himself a people of his own. It seems that this is evident today among the different people groups in the world, as well as different cultural dynamics within any particular people group. Having taught overseas for many years, I now see different cultures in different places on the ethical continuum. The joy I now receive is in using my gifting (including my education) to help different people groups grasp new and fresh ideas that impact their culture in keeping with God's design. This is true in my own church as well as I see people in different places on the ethical continuum. Therefore, the story of redemption is *itself* a model of healthy church life!

What this all means is that our interpretation and decisions should be consistent with the theological development of the Bible as it unfolds. Since the ethics of Scripture (as captured by the stories, applications, and commands) demonstrate development, the way we use Scripture in our various contexts should demonstrate similar sensitivity and patience to the complex issues with which we are faced.

Chapter 6

BRINGING THE KINGDOM
INTO OUR PRESENT WORLD

I teach a Doctor of Ministry course in which the students, many of whom are pastors, have to evaluate plateaued or declining churches as part of developing a model to evaluate their own organizations. They are required to observe other churches and report back on what they have observed from these other churches. The list of fails is breathtaking to say the least. Imagine visiting a church, being the first one to arrive on site as a visitor, sitting in a chair in an empty sanctuary, and being asked by the usher to move to another chair because that particular chair is "their" chair. Or, visiting a church and all the main doors are locked, only to find out they only unlock the door in the rear since no one uses the front doors anymore. Or, visiting a church where nothing has changed since 1960 (pews, sanctuary color, programming, and so on). Or, as one student quipped, visiting a church that was 250 years old... and some of the original members were still there! If the kingdom of God "is what God is doing in this world *through the community of faith for the redemptive plans of God*" what happened to these churches?[200]

Our fifth principle is that *our interpretation and decisions should bring the eschatological kingdom—the true kingdom of Jesus—into our present world.* Where possible, our decisions should bring features of the eschatological kingdom out into our present world so that the surrounding culture can more clearly see God's mission being fulfilled. This is what is behind Christ's words about the will of God being done on earth as it is in heaven (the Lord's Prayer). Another way of saying this is that applications, rituals, and traditions done well bring Christ into clear focus now, while these same behaviors done poorly shield others from the truth and in some cases simply make them feel good. A note of caution here—the Bible also demonstrates that when a practice leads to offense, care should be given before moving ahead. In this chapter, we are asking, "Does our interpretation and applications bring the eschatological Kingdom into our present world?"

The Present Problem

Kevin Vanhoozer begins his helpful work, *The Drama of Doctrine*, with the claim that the gospel is "intrinsically dramatic."[201] This metaphor enables him to establish essential links between theology (dramaturgy), Scripture (the script), theological understanding (performance), the church (the company), and the pastor (director). This ties together much of what I have argued throughout this study. Assigning the role of the church to the company of actors identifies a key responsibility of why church exists in the first place. Willem VanGemeren argues similarly when he states, "[Jesus'] kingdom rule in the church is not a limitation of his kingship but rather a *manifestation* of his rule."[202] In other words, we play a significant role in revealing God and his work to a lost and tired world.

This surfaces key aspects of the church that many Christians overlook today. In my experience, most Christians are simply trying to survive life and have no real concept of the important role that they—individually and together—play in revealing the kingdom to the people around them. Why is this so and what is the impact?

As discussed earlier, in 1993, Wells argued that evangelicalism had lost its way. Specifically, he argued that two models of pastoral ministry had dominated evangelicalism in the twentieth century. One model focused on theology as *doctrinal truth* whereby theology had largely become irrelevant. The other model focused on *professionalism* wherein practical needs arose from the demands of the pastorate and therefore theology had become peripheral.[203] While there is much truth in this assessment, this is only part of the picture.

Aside from the deceptiveness of sin, my experience has revealed that at a very basic level, the decline of the church is partly the result of the insidious combination of a weak and ineffective understanding of doctrine and truth combined with the very powerful ability of sin to distract. When I mention a weak and ineffective understanding of doctrine, I am not speaking about more teaching on dogma. Rather, it involves an engagement with theology that is both life-giving and overcomes what Vanhoozer refers to as the "fateful dichotomy between doctrine and life." He further adds that "he who is tired of doctrine is tired of life, for doctrine *is* the stuff of life."[204]

As we discussed earlier, whenever we have a conversation about God, we are engaging in theology. And *every one of our conversations* should be life-giving, whether we are exposing the destructiveness of sin or painting a hopeful picture of the future in Christ. As Vanhoozer argues, "To introduce the question of doctrine is to raise the question of the content of Christian preaching. Where doctrine is weak and ambiguous, so is preaching, and speech about God in general."[205] For the sake of the church and for the individuals—Christians and non-Christians alike—who attend and hear sermons, we must find better ways of communicating the core truths of our beliefs into the lives of others so that what they are hearing leads them to greater hunger and thirst for God as well as a greater desire to realize authentic hope in their present lives.

I still remember the day when I stood up to give my sermon and looked out over the congregation and was startled by what I saw. After numerous conversations with many in the congregation on all matters including personal sin, excitements, blessings, challenges, and so on, I saw them with different eyes. I *knew* who was sleeping with whom, who was struggling with alcohol abuse, who was struggling with pornography addiction, whose teens were engaging in immoral actions, and so on.

I stood there with a profound sense of responsibility as I looked at the flock and silently pleaded with God to help me. I stood there long enough that some began to cough discreetly to remind me that I was supposed to give a sermon. While I had long ago learned to depend on the Spirit for the words to say, on that Sunday I *depended* on the Spirit in ways much deeper than before. This led me to ask why these people came to church in the first place. I knew that, contrary to earlier generations, it was not out of duty as there are way too many distractions in today's world for this to occur. Rather, it was because of a strong desire that there was something better than what they were experiencing in life. This is why the church exists! To give *people*, who live in the midst of a very cruel, sinful, broken, tired, and distracted world genuine hope for something better. This is the beginning of living out the kingdom.

The Kingdom of God

So, what is the kingdom of God? At the risk of being overly simple, many in our churches need a working idea. At a very simple level, the kingdom in Jesus' world would have meant "a people governed by a king."[206] To help us in our decision-making process, a more nuanced definition will demonstrate how the church is to function as part of this kingdom.

To begin, the kingdom is about people, but not just any people. It is made up of those people who are redeemed and ruled by Jesus. This differentiates the church from all other organizations. And, these people are defined by a particular ethic, or way of thinking and living. Understanding this basic ethic is essential for determining how our decisions help or hinder both our testimony and our impact in our local cultures.

A key element of this kingdom ethic is fellowship and community.[207] Some of the images include "vineyard, branches and vines and wine, a 'nation,' a fellowship at table, a 'people,' and 'Israel'; they are also a flock, and they are 'one,' friends, children of God, a brotherhood, and a family."

These metaphors reveal much about the nature of this community. It is to be a genuine and authentic community. It is to be a community nourished on relationship with each other and with Jesus. It is to be a community that shares things in common for the benefit of all involved.

Another key aspect of this kingdom ethic is being set apart. But being set apart carries with it great responsibility. Matthew 17:24–27 provides an example of how being set apart functions within society. In this passage, Peter is challenged by tax collectors when he is asked, "Doesn't your teacher pay the temple tax?" In the ensuing conversation between Peter and Jesus, it becomes clear that "kings do not tax their children... but their subjects. Accordingly, Jesus, as the unique Son of God, is greater than the temple and is exempt from paying this tax to his Father's house."[208] And yet, Jesus decides to pay the temple tax to avoid creating offense (Matt. 17:27). While Jesus was not above offending the Pharisees on occasion, here a key principle arises in that he was not willing to offend his fellow Jews who were part of the system. "All decisions are made on the basis of what enhances the gospel, and Christ's ambassadors are to surrender their 'rights' for its sake."[209]

The Temple as an Example of Kingdom Work

If the kingdom fundamentally is people who are under the rule of Jesus doing the work of Jesus, how does this help us understand our role as churches within our various cultural contexts? At its core it means that the church is the dwelling place of God. Just as earlier we discussed the metaphors of the Jewish priesthood and sacrificial system to help us understand Christ and our roles as Christians, the authors of the New Testament similarly used the metaphor of temple (1 Cor. 3:16). How are we to define this temple, which is now spiritual, and how does this help us? Having taught in several other countries are we to define it by looking at Hindu or Buddhist temples? Or perhaps the other temples of the Roman era? While these other temple systems provide some help, I believe looking at the Jewish temple is more helpful.

In the Corinthian church "there is clear evidence of Jews and Gentile synagogue adherents among the Corinthian Christians."[210] Ben Witherington explains further, "Because early Christianity had neither priests nor temples nor sacrifices, to the outsider a household assembly would surely have seemed much more like a social club, a society, or a group of students gathered around a great teacher teaching in the home of his patron, than like a religious group."[211] Since Paul used the metaphors of priesthood and sacrifice to explain Christ's fulfillment of the Old Testament, it is not unreasonable that he also used Jewish temple imagery as well.

When the Jewish temple is viewed as the background, this metaphor comes alive in fresh ways as we can then understand that there is much more to the metaphor than simply God's dwelling. "For Paul the imagery reflects the OT people of God. Although they are never called God's temple as such, they are God's own people, among whom God chose to 'dwell' by tabernacling in their midst."[212] "Remarkably, Paul believes that even these badly mixed-up Christians are still God's temple where God still dwells."[213]

Therefore, the temple metaphor begins to define more precisely what it means to bring the kingdom of God out into our own cultures. Almost all major commentaries note that the use of plurals (you yourselves) come together in the singular (God's temple). And this one temple is occupied by God himself in the form of the Spirit. This was God's plan all along, to dwell among his people.

Similarly, Paul used the temple imagery in Ephesians 2:19–22. Even more than in the Corinthians Epistles, the emphasis on Jew and Gentile relations is very pronounced. Paul argued here that God had created an entirely new humanity (singular) by reconciling the Jews and Gentiles. This is the context for him to claim that the Gentiles are now "fellow citizens" and "members of his household" (Eph. 2:19). This is also the context for him to claim that this new group "rises to become a holy temple in the Lord" (Eph. 2:21). "According to Old Testament prophecy the temple at Jerusalem was to be the place where all nations at the end time would come to worship and pray to the living God (Isa. 66:18–20; cf. Isa. 2:1–5; Mic. 4:1–5). The temple imagery here is to be understood in fulfilment of these promises. Now through Christ, Gentiles have been brought near to God, and along with Jews they have become the new temple, the place where God's presence dwells."[214]

So, what does all of this mean? What if we can catch a glimpse of what it means to be the temple of God in our various cultures today by looking at the functions and ministries performed in the Jewish temple? For example, the sacrifices were offered in the Jewish temple. As we discussed earlier, as priests we are to offer up spiritual sacrifices which are pleasing to God. When the world looks at the church, the spiritual temple, do they see us offering these sacrifices, especially on behalf of others? Also as discussed earlier, the priests at the Jewish temple were to mediate for the people, accept their sacrifices, and bless them. When the world looks at the church, do they see Christians caring and mediating for, and blessing the people who come?

Another function of the Jewish temple was the celebration of the major festivals. For example, the Festival of Tabernacles was seven days long (Deut. 16:13–17). The opening verse is an invitation to celebrate this festival. Daniel Block explains that there were two reasons for this festival.[215] It provided the Israelites an occasion to celebrate their sense of community in a festival of joy. Second, as it was at the end of the agricultural cycle, it also provided the Israelites an opportunity for corporate thanksgiving in the presence of God. In this regard, the Israelites were told to "be joyful at your festival" (Deut. 16:14).

This festival played a major role in Jesus' ministry as recorded in John 7–8. Francis Moloney argues that joy and celebration were at the center of this festival.[216] It was marked by singing, dancing, celebrations of life and light, the enjoyment of God's blessings, and so on. "This celebration lasted most of the night for each of the seven days of the feast."[217] So when the world looks at the church, do they see the worship, singing, dancing, joy, and so on, that characterized the festivals?

Gospel Impulses of the Kingdom

If we assume that one of the reasons these temple functions were instituted was to create a corporate heart of remembrance and joy among the Israelites, and give them opportunities to celebrate and express this corporate heart, this might give us insight into why the church is to function as a temple in today's world. When we look at the spiritual temple, we see a similar dynamic occurring as with the Jewish Temple. We already know that joy is part of the fruit of the Spirit (Gal. 5:22). But more to the point, Jesus alerted the disciples that after he left, the Spirit would teach them all things and remind them of everything he had been telling them (John 14:26). As Moloney argues, "The teaching of the Holy Spirit recalls what Jesus has said, *taking it deeper and farther into the memory and consciousness of the disciples* of Jesus."[218]

This immediately raises several questions. What are these deeper impulses that are driven into our hearts? When and how do we, as Christians today, "push the envelope" to bring these deeper impulses into our various cultures? When do we show restraint and work to avoid offense? In other words, we are asking the fundamental question, "What does it mean to represent God to a broken world?" This is a challenging quest because we are now living in a clash of kingdoms; God and Caesar.[219]

As we argued in the last chapter, God is moving historically and consistently in culture to bring about redemption. Through the work of Christ to bring about forgiveness of sins and the indwelling ministry of the Spirit the church now has a new paradigm based on love. But it is more detailed than that. We share something in common with our fellow humans and should care deeply about bringing to them the truth of the Christian message in life-giving ways. This means that we, as kingdom citizens, should be "compelled by love to 'good deeds' or 'doing good' in the public sector" for the common good.[220]

Remember, the connection between Church and world is by no means accidental. "The Church's relationship to the world is determinative for her *authentic vocation*."[221] This means that the church becomes the transforming agent of the world. Thus, the church represents the true hope and destiny of all of creation. In other words, the church, as a kingdom entity, pioneers "the future of all mankind."[222] Or, as Paul states in Ephesians 3:21, "to him be the glory *in the church* and in Christ Jesus throughout all generations, for ever and ever!" But how does this happen?

With the indwelling Spirit, the church now has "gospel impulses"[223] that are growing in us as we mature. These are "core values" that should define who we are, especially in contrast to the surrounding world. Grenz argues that religion plays a vital role in developing specific societal forms, and that each religion can and should be assessed specifically on the social structures that they foster and develop.[224] This surfaces the question, "Which [religious] vision provides the basis for community in the truest sense?"[225] This is one of the core questions that leadership in the church should ask as they make decisions. So, what are these gospel impulses, or core values? While not exhaustive, there are several that should shape our approach to bringing the kingdom to our world through our decision-making.

First, as discussed earlier we should always demonstrate respect and dignity to our fellow citizens. Every human is worthy of our respect, precisely because of their God-given dignity, no matter the nature of their sin and struggle! By now, hopefully it is clear that dignity trumps confrontation. Since none of us have the ability to convict, redeem, or transform another, our focus should be on loving patience and waiting on the Spirit to carry out his role. Only then can we fulfill our role of helping others around us. This does not mean we are silent. On the contrary, it means that our fellow humans have such dignity that we need to appropriately and honestly discuss the challenges and issues of their lives and our societies.

Second, we should unwaveringly commit to sexual morality as a means of demonstrating respect and relational care. At its core, sexual morality is an exercise in demonstrating respect for others precisely because of their dignity. In light of this, marriage can be defined simply as the ability to love and minister to a spouse in more intimate and significant ways than any other human. Paul argues that "the wife does not have authority over her own body but yields it to her husband. In the same way, the husband does not have authority over his own body but yields it to his wife" (1 Cor. 7:4).

When placed in its cultural context, the effect is breathtaking. We are in relationship to care for and bring joy to each other. This is why Paul can begin this argument with the exhortation to flee sexual immorality (1 Cor. 6:18; cf, 1 Cor. 7:2). After countless conversations with many people involved in sexual immorality, I can say with confidence that immorality is self-centered, degrading and relationally destructive. Those that have developed their marriages along God's design are the ones who begin to experience the authentic joy he envisioned.

Third, we should be committed to culture care. In other words, we should genuinely be concerned about our society and how we can impact it for good. It is well known that, when God sent Judah into exile, he commanded them to "seek the peace and prosperity of the city to which I have carried you into exile. Pray to the Lord for it, because if it prospers, you too will prosper" (Jer. 29:7). Throughout my life, I have long been sensitive to the friction created in my own country due to the political divide. As Christians we should be very careful about engaging in the vitriolic, degrading, and hateful criticisms leveled on both sides of the political divide. As one whose sermons are on-line, I am very familiar with how far the internet allows us to "throw stones" at those who's messages we dislike or disagree with. On the contrary, we should do all that we can to partner with those organizations that share similar values, whether or not they are Christian.

While there are many others that could be discussed, these are sufficient to illustrate how our growing Spirit-led intuition becomes valuable if, together, we follow our "hunches." These gospel impulses are part of the good news that we both believe in and live out. As Grenz argues,

"The divine design is that we mirror within creation what God is like in God's own eternal reality."[226]

The "Now—Not Yet" of the Kingdom

Having identified several key gospel impulses that are now shaping our thinking, it is worth asking how earlier Christians lived out these impulses in their own communities. A related question is, "What happened when culture did not allow for advancement of these gospel impulses?" While we may have freedom, we are not free to do as we please, as Paul makes clear in Galatians 5:13–26. Our freedom is to be used for the glory of God, and even more specifically, the creation of a community of God's people.

The early Christians of the first century had the daunting task of navigating between the laws and expectations of the various cultures in which they lived, and the new principles of the kingdom that now described their lives. In this context, they seemed to expect the Lord's return at any moment. As discussed earlier, in many cases the authors of the New Testament encouraged the early Christians to practice some degree of conservatism for the sake of living out the kingdom within their own communities.

This daunting task and the resulting tensions are what scholars refer to when they talk about the "now—not yet" theology presented in the New Testament. As was true then, we live in both the "now" and yet we are very aware of the "not yet" that is to come. This is partly what Paul is getting at when he claims that "God raised us up with Christ and seated us with him in the heavenly realms in Christ Jesus" (Eph. 2:6). Here is that "clash" of kingdoms we discussed earlier. Or as Peter O'Brien states, in Paul's theology "the resurrection of believers with Christ has already taken place."[227] And yet, we still have to navigate a very complex and as yet an un-redeemed world.

For the sake of the gospel, it would make sense for the early Christian leaders to encourage social conservatism when necessary and boldness when possible. The marriage text in Ephesians 5:21–33 represents a view of marriage unheard of in the ancient world. It demonstrated respect to both spouses in a world in which little freedom was granted. And yet, Paul encouraged conservatism in 1 Thessalonians 4:10–12 in order to "win the respect of outsiders." Similarly, Paul taught that in Christ there is no slave (Gal. 3:28), and yet he encouraged conservatism in Ephesians 6:5–8.

While there are many other examples, I believe this surfaces a principle that helps us in our decision-making today. With our freedom, we have a responsibility to use this freedom to further God's mission and bring the kingdom out into our world. If that means we can push the cultural envelope, we should do so. If it means that we will offend culture, we should show restraint. In other words, how far can we go and still make the gospel attractive? The answer to this question is unique to each culture.

Summary

When we understand that we are people ruled by Jesus and that we have a different ethic that differentiates us from the world, we begin to think differently. Our love should motivate us, as churches, to move into the lives of others as well as the community at-large. But how we move into those lives is critical for the sake of the kingdom. If we are to fully live out the Lord's prayer that the kingdom of God would come as it is in heaven, then we need to more fully grasp the principles behind kingdom living.

As our conversations and sermons about God become more life-giving, first, we increasingly become people who attract others to our beliefs (Titus 2:9–10). As Christopher Wright argues, we become attractors—not attractors to ourselves but to the God we serve.[228] It means that we begin to wrestle with and understand our own congregations better and work to create safe spaces for them to wrestle with the Spirit and allow him to do his work.

But second, it means more than that. It also means that we more fully grasp our responsibility and privilege of being a people set apart with a unique ethic to accomplish an incredible mission—the mission of God. As we work to trust the Spirit, our collective gospel impulses become more reliable and realistic, such that we begin to more naturally think about how to bring the kingdom out to our respective cultures.

Finally, when we balance our freedoms in Christ with our love for our cultures, we begin to look for and find ways to live in society in life-changing ways. As Christians we become more acutely aware of the tension between the present (now) and the hope of glory (not yet). This means we learn to be bold where we can be and conservative and sensitive where we need to be, all for the sake of mission. If our primary mission is to reach the nations for Christ, then failure to push the envelope results in a plateaued or declining church, while pushing too hard results in an offended culture.

Back to the students in the DMin course. What they learned through the exercise was that the churches they evaluated largely avoided change and boldness. Rather, these churches' tendencies were to protect themselves and stick to rituals and traditions which had been established long ago. As a result, there was very little decision-making that took culture and the mission of God into account.

What this all means is that our interpretation and decisions should bring the eschatological kingdom—the true kingdom of Jesus—into our present world, so that the surrounding culture can more clearly see God's mission being fulfilled. In other words, all of our applications, rituals, and traditions should be done well in order to bring Christ into clear focus now, while avoiding doing these same behaviors poorly and risk shielding others from the truth.

Chapter 7

CREATING A FLOURISHING FAITH COMMUNITY

S oon after I assumed the role of senior pastor at my church, the elders became aware that there was a couple who had started to file for divorce. When they brought it to my attention they were surprised that, not only was I aware of the situation, but I had never informed the elders even though I had been working with the couple and had even helped them get into marriage counseling... all to no avail. The elders' experience had taught them that people living in "sin" needed to be brought to the elders for proper "handling." I informed them that, using that criteria, they had better get ready because the line would be blocks long. As we began to discuss the concept of sin, we agreed that sin alone was never the reason to bring a couple before the elders, specifically because Jesus clarified that sin was much more invasive than behavior (Matt. 5–7).

After studying the Scriptures, we agreed that we would bring before the elders those whose sin was destructive to the unity of the church; namely if they were boasting about their sin, teaching doctrine against our statement of faith, or otherwise dividing the church. In the meantime, the much healthier approach to helping people with sin or struggles required a more personal, patient, and hands-on approach. The core of effectively helping others required that we develop a culture of flourishing, rather than a transactional culture of addressing sin.

This leads us to our sixth and final principle: *our interpretation and decisions should lead to a flourishing community of faith.* If our behaviors do not lead to a flourishing community, hypocrisy results and the mission of God is not fulfilled. Here a flourishing community is defined primarily as the consistent and proper integration of our confessional (stated) theology with our functional (lived) theology. In every case where Scripture highlights discrepancies in this area, problems surface. It is crucial for churches to filter their practices through this lens to ensure their communities flourish. In this chapter, we are answering the question, "Does our interpretation and decisions lead to a thriving and growing community of faith?" While the last chapter focused on the outward expression of the kingdom, this chapter focuses on the necessary inner dynamic of health.

Introduction

As we explore this final principle, the best place to start is with Jeremiah's letter to the exiles who had been carried off to Babylon (Jer. 29:1–9). This letter lays a surprising foundation for what it means to be in the public sector and the role played by the people of God. This then allows us to grasp what a healthy culture looks like. To understand the significance of this passage, it is helpful to grasp the background.[229] The letter was written to those taken into exile along with King Jehoiachin (597 BC).

Apparently, several prophets made announcements, supposedly in the name of the Lord, about the demise of Babylon and the quick return of the exiles to Judah (Jer. 29:8–9, 15, 21–28). These supposed prophecies were provoking the community, and Jeremiah encouraged the people not to believe them as they were false prophecies (Jer. 29:8–9). It is against these prophets that Jeremiah stood up and declared the truth about their exile in Babylon. In contrast to the false prophecies,

Jeremiah made it clear that their stay in Babylon would actually last decades (Jer. 25:12).

What was new and surprising in this letter of Jeremiah were the instructions for their stay in exile. They were to "build houses and settle down." The further evidence of their longer stay was expressed in that they were to plant gardens, marry and have children, and increase in number while in Babylon. Within this context, Jeremiah further exhorted them to "seek the peace and prosperity of the city" to which God exiled them (Jer. 29:7). The reason given is that if the city prospers, so will they!

While Nebuchadnezzar was the "historical agent" who captured the people and brought them to Babylon, Jeremiah made it clear that it was actually the work of God himself.[230] Exile was shown not to be the end of God's people, but the beginning of a new era. As J. A. Thompson argues, "Jeremiah by these words cast the people completely adrift from all those things on which they depended and which they regarded as essential to their own well-being, a nation-state, kingship, an army, national borders, the temple. Without all these Yahweh could give the nation new perspectives and a new understanding of their calling."[231]

The triple use of shalom in this passage "implicitly recalls the earlier claims of Jeremiah's prophetic rivals that Yahweh would bring about for Judah not a bad fate but peace."[232] How ironic that peace would indeed occur, but not at home! Rather, peace would occur on enemy territory. The exiles are told to accept this judgment, settle down, and work for the good of the enemy!

Christopher Wright argues that this is an example of the ongoing mission of God—the Abrahamic mission of being a blessing to the nations. Later on, Daniel and his three friends were shown to exemplify Jeremiah's exhortation. They settled down in Babylon and worked in government service. Indeed, Nebuchadnezzar could find no one equal to Daniel and his friends (Dan. 1:18–20). They were model citizens, hardworking, and were distinguished for their trustworthiness and integrity.

A Flourishing Community

The stories of Jeremiah and Daniel raise the question of a flourishing community and the role that this type of community plays in the lives of the individuals within the community as well as the broader society. Wolfhart Pannenberg asks an intriguing question, "How might Jesus' teaching be understood as a revolution in ethical thought, leading to a permanent reconstruction of our ethical foundation?"[233] This should be the quest of every church leadership team.

I agree with McKnight when he states, "kingdom mission as church mission means the kingdom citizen is compelled by love to 'good deeds' or 'doing good' in the public sector."[234] But is it possible to live life this way if our church cultures are not healthy and flourishing? I answer with a resounding "no!" "To be blessed is to be ushered into an endless life of flourishing in the best sense of happiness." In other words, God's blessing ushers us into a "new reality of unstoppable, ever-intensifying, and glorious joy, pleasure, and happiness."[235] I believe this is the direct result of creating a safe, redemptive—flourishing—culture as discussed earlier.

Volf further argues that in order for flourishing to occur, "we need to *make plausible* the claim that the love of God and of neighbor is the key."[236] In other words, in order to create a flourishing church, the *experience* of those in church needs to match the theology taught by the church.

The opposite of this is hollowing out from within where hypocrisy begins to define the church culture. In other words, we say one thing but subtly mean another. For example, we preach and teach that we should show grace to those struggling with sexual immorality, but sometimes the reality is that they are unwelcome in our churches. I have heard this very complaint many times in all of my discussions with those who no longer attend church.

In Vanhoozer's drama analogy, the concept of being "real" plays a critical role. "Theology has nothing to do with illusion or with pretending to be something one is not. On the contrary, theology exhorts the faithful *to become something they already are*—to participate in the eschatological reality of the coming kingdom of God."[237] There is no shortcut to authenticity. It is very difficult and challenging to create a culture defined by authenticity... and it begins with the pastors, elders, and other leaders. Where transparency is lacking in leadership, authenticity is also lacking.

I still remember the day when my youngest child, as a teenager, stated that every time he saw a preacher or teacher, he was wondering what they were hiding that would soon come to light. This was at the end of a year when several of our pastoral acquaintances had been exposed as sexually immoral. There is very little more crushing to a dad who has committed his life to authentic pastoral ministry than to have his teenage child begin to lose respect for church leaders and suspect them of relational fraud. And I am not alone. This is crushing for anyone who has placed some degree of trust in their spiritual leaders. Hypocrisy is destructive! So, what is the answer?

The Role of Joy in Flourishing

Before we get to authenticity, we first have to discuss the role of joy in a flourishing community. To begin, Christianity is a unique religion of joy.[238] The Israelites were commanded to celebrate their festivals with joy (Deut. 16:14). David knew that joy was found in God's presence (1 Chron. 16:27; Ps. 16:11). Even the psalmist cries out that all of creation is to express joy (Ps. 96:11–13). When Mary found out she was pregnant, she began her song with rejoicing (Luke 1:46–47). Similarly, the story of Jesus' birth was announced to the angels in terms of joy (Luke 2:10–11). Paul exhorts us to "Rejoice in the Lord always. I will say it again: Rejoice!" (Phil. 4:4). And there are many more such passages.

But how can we demonstrate and experience joy with so much suffering in the world, especially when the universal symbol of Christianity is the cross? In fact, interwoven among these passages about joy are many passages about suffering. And yet, joy is a central message of the Bible. How can these work together? In answering these difficult questions, it is helpful to distinguish between joy and fun. Whereas fun is fleeting and serves amusement, joy is an enduring quality that marks "one's attitude toward living."[239] In this regard, we were created for joy. This is why joy is listed as part of the fruit of the Spirit (Gal. 5:22).

Here, Marianne Maye Thompson is helpful when she distinguishes two types of joy. One is related to elation and celebration and the other is a "disposition manifested in the midst of affliction and distress."[240] One is joy *because of* one's experiences and the other is joy *notwithstanding* one's condition. Both are grounded in an authentic and life-giving relationship with God.

Both aspects of joy serve a critical role in Christian theology. "Joy in life's happiness motivates us to revolt against the life that is destroyed and against those that destroy life."[241] This should lead to a deep hope for liberation from suffering to joy. As a result, "we don't accuse God because there is suffering in the world. Rather, we protest in the name of God against suffering and those who cause it."[242]

This tension between deep dissatisfaction and genuine hope accounts for the Christian message that joy can be experienced throughout life. Joy is more than a feeling; it is a genuine emotion that is tied to how one perceives reality.[243] This principle lies behind genuine faith. Our faith is based on our belief that there is one true living God who can be trusted in all things.

Volf argues further that "maybe the most difficult challenge for Christians it to actually *believe* that God is fundamental to human flourishing... *That*, I think, is today's most fundamental challenge for theologians, priests, and ministers, and Christian lay people: to *really mean* that the presence and activity of the God of love, who can make us love our neighbors as ourselves, is our hope and the hope of the world."[244]

A Model of Authenticity

This raises the question of authenticity. I am convinced that the road to authenticity is also the road to creating a flourishing community. And the road to authenticity is the same road which more effectively brings the kingdom out into our various cultures. The starting point is to identify the culture by which each church desires to be defined. Many churches and organizations confuse what should be *measured* and what should be *managed*. For example, is a church to be evaluated by the transformation that is occurring or by the number of attendees?

Authenticity requires that we take stock of the actual culture we are building in our churches and then manage toward the culture we desire. If we want to be a loving culture, then ask the marginalized if we are loving. If we want to be a generous culture, then ask the poor if we are generous. If we want to be a safe and redemptive church, then ask those struggling with sin if we are safe and redemptive. If we want to partner well with our communities, then ask the community leaders how we might partner together and if we are partnering together well. "The point of our lives is not to get smart or to get rich or even to get happy. The point is to discover God's purposes for us and to make them our own. The point is to learn ways of loving God above all and our neighbor as ourselves."[245] Happiness then becomes a by-product of developing a healthy and flourishing community.

As discussed earlier, the pathways leading to redemption are winding and often go backward. None of us have the capacity to convict, redeem, or transform. Every person's life journey toward the cross is a long and winding road that requires great patience on the part of those leading and watching. It is far easier to be critical of others than ourselves. And yet, the truth is that we are redeemed to be redemptive toward others. We are blessed to be a blessing toward others. We have been shown generosity so that we can be generous toward others.

So, how do we do this? By working to surface and identify that reality by which we want to be defined. Here is where the Bible is invaluable. It lays out the dynamics and characteristics of the kingdom that should define us, starting with a deep love and respect for every human (and creation), no matter their struggle. Once that cultural identity is defined, then we must do the hard work of looking at all aspects of organizational life and behavior in order to address those areas where we are not congruent with our cultural ideal.

It means we must take a long and hard look at the differences between our stated beliefs (our confessions) and our lived-out beliefs (our actual individual and organization lifestyle). This is one of the greatest challenges in leadership! If we believe that we should not grumble or complain, do we grumble and complain? If we believe that we should show grace, do we get impatient and angry? If we believe that only the Holy Spirit can convict a person of sin, do we manipulate and begin to exercise control over others? The answers to these questions illustrate only the beginning of what it means to develop a culture that is redemptive, safe, reflective of God's grace, and attractive and inviting to the outside world.

Also, as alluded to above, this cannot be self-diagnosed. It can only be seen clearly through the eyes of others. Just as we cannot see ourselves clearly, a church struggles to see itself clearly as well. This is why it is important that we ask the recipients of our love how they view our church. I think every church should regularly ponder the question, "If we shut our doors today, would our neighbors be glad, sad, or even notice?" There is only one appropriate and healthy answer to this question, and *it can only be answered by our neighbors*!

As those educated in the more technical parts of leadership know, such as organizational behavior, relational entropy is a very real dynamic that plagues all organizations. In other words, our natural tendency is to divide, which follows nicely Satan's most powerful ability to deceive. Church cultures do not naturally develop along healthy lines. They must be shepherded and guided carefully (Ps. 78:72).

The world is replete with examples of businesses where the stated values on the wall do not match the operational values that actually define the organization. Accordingly, the world is replete with organizations and churches that are relationally unhealthy. There are numerous tools to evaluate these dynamics, but the hard work involves *actually changing* the organizational behaviors and qualities that define the organization to more consistently reflect the values desired by leadership and the church.

I love to remind our church and our leadership teams that, while it is Jesus' church, we also play a huge role in defining our own culture. Therefore, we must dream, and dream big. For example, for our student ministries, we remind the parents that it is *their* teens we are discussing. What are their hopes and dreams for their teens? Dream the impossible, as that is where God loves to operate. Our responsibility as leaders is to help these parents and teens together realize their dreams.

Vision that is honoring to the Holy Spirit starts from the ground up... not the top down! Using the example of student ministries, the dreams and hopes of the parents is a far more powerful starting point for developing vision than that of the elders or pastors. Our ministry plans and goals should be the summary of the dreams of everyone in our church, not the dream of the senior pastor or elders.

This means that all of our interpretations and decisions should lead to a healthy, flourishing, and authentic community. As Christopher Wright argues, this allows us to serve our priestly responsibility of being a people who represent God to the world[246] *and* a people who attract others to God.[247] And, as Volf argued earlier, this is perhaps the greatest challenge facing Christian leadership today.

A Final Word

This cannot be accomplished simply by excellent preaching, although that is important. The culture of the church is reflective of the lives of the people in the church. As they live authentic Christian lives, there is a much greater congruency between what they say they believe and how they actually live life. This leads to greater joy and more significant impact in each local culture as the church becomes a trusted place of ministry.

Just as important, this is what we were made for. Jesus, in his final celebration at the Festival of Tabernacles, amazes the Jews such that they become inquisitive of his source of learning (John 7:15). Jesus replies that "anyone who chooses to do the will of God will find out whether my teaching comes from God or whether I speak on my own" (John 7:17). In other words, as Moloney argues, "Those *genuinely* seeking to do the will of God will be able to make their decision about the origins of Jesus' teaching."[248]

Similarly, shortly after that Jesus said to those "who had believed him... If you hold to my teaching, you are really my disciples. Then you will know the truth, and the truth will set you free" (John 8:31–32). While the second part of this verse is widely known, the first part is critical for our discussion. True freedom comes through obeying Jesus' teachings. It is not an exercise in better knowledge, but an exercise in more faithful living.

What these verses teach us is that we were created all along to live like Christ. It is significantly more than simply knowing the truth... it is living the truth. This is the source of faith, confidence, and joy. It is the ultimate paradox of faithfully enduring suffering, which leads to deeper joy, which leads to bringing the kingdom into the lives of those we care about in authentic ways. This was the "center" that Grenz was arguing for when he stated that the task facing the church today is returning the church to the generous orthodoxy for which it was created. "It means returning a truly evangelical theology to the center of the church for the sake of the church's mission as a worshiping community of people sent into the world with the gospel."[249]

Again, this cannot be done simply through excellent preaching. It must include much patience with people who struggle daily with sin. It is accomplished one at a time, often through one-on-one encounters where the destructiveness of sin and the reality of Christ are discussed openly in a safe and trusting environment. It requires much patience and commitment to walk with people through the various mazes in which they find themselves. Building this kind of church culture takes a long time.

Summary

As we turn our gaze to our surrounding culture, it is critical that we first take stock of our own internal organizational health. The health (prosperity and peace) of our surrounding culture and our ability to genuinely share the love of Christ is dependent on our health as a church. There is no shortcut to this health. It begins with the individuals in our churches which, when they experience redemption in their own lives, adds up to a powerful dynamic group of people who are able to bring blessing to those around them whom they love.

This is accomplished through generating a flourishing church which is defined by both redemption and safety. When these two come together people naturally move toward great health which results in living out faith in authentic ways. At the heart of this endeavor is the gradual and slow movement of bringing our actual lived-out theology in line with our stated, or confessional, theology. Where these are misaligned, hypocrisy is obvious and either pushes people away or makes them hide in shame. Conversely, where these are aligned, joy and trust are present in a unique way that invites people closer in their walk with Jesus.

What this all means is that our interpretation and decisions should lead to a flourishing community of faith. If our decisions do not lead to a thriving community of faith, we should reevaluate both our interpretation and resulting decisions. The way to measure this is to ask those who are the recipients of our ministries. Simply preaching good sermons will not create this type of environment. It is a combination of personal ministry combined with effective preaching and teaching. Therefore, all of our interpretation and decisions should lead to a thriving and flourishing community of faith.

Chapter 8

TYING IT ALL TOGETHER

W
e've come a long way since asking our original question of what freedom the Bible gives us to live out our Christian principles and theology in any particular context, while still maintaining faithfulness to Scripture. We have covered a vast terrain of subjects, ideas, principles of theology, and so on. It is time to summarize the key points and tie it all together.

Introduction

We began by arguing that the Bible is rarely clear when dealing with the challenges of the 21st century. Pastors and church leaders are faced with this dilemma on a regular basis and must make decisions "on the fly" about people, their relationships, their struggles with sin, and so on. This is also true of church leaderships in different cultural situations. They must regularly make decisions that navigate the tensions between their theological beliefs and traditions, the realities of their various cultures, and the expectations of their people. In most of these scenarios, the Bible is rarely clear in its direction and application.

In this context I proposed what I believe to be a much needed decision-making method that takes into account the actual problems needing addressed, the Holy Spirit-driven intuition of those impacted by the decision, the framing of the problem with appropriate biblical and theological principles, and the necessary steps to decide how the

Bible might shape the decisions. As decisions are proposed using this method, a framework of interpretation is needed to both guide the process as well as safeguard the decisions and ensure faithfulness is accomplished.

Chapter 1 – Using Methods and Models

In this chapter I proposed a model of how to approach Scripture in cases where direct application is not evident. We developed the model by analyzing patterns in Scripture wherein adjustments or departures from the law were evident. The foundation for each of these examples was the assumption that, in each case, there was a higher principle at work which both allowed and mandated that better solutions were needed. The clearest example was the example of Jesus himself in Matthew 12 regarding violations of the Sabbath.

The key principles included, first, that with the coming of the New Covenant, a new order has been instituted which allows for a broader application of our theological convictions. Second, with the indwelling Holy Spirit, the experiences of the people of God play an increasing role in discerning the guidance of the Spirit. Third, human freedom involves interpreting Scripture in keeping with the mission of God. Fourth, the church should take seriously Peter's warning about not testing God. Jesus himself provided a paradigm-shifting approach to bringing Scripture to bear in healthy ways in various contexts. Finally, the ultimate priority is to express a love for people that matches God's own deep and sacrificial love.

Chapter 2 – Expressing God's Love for a Broken World

In this chapter I identified our first principle that *all of our interpretations and decisions should lead to bringing God's love out to this broken world.* In our decision-making scheme, we are considering both the Spirit-led informed intuition of the group alongside of looking at multiple possible decisions based on our interpretation of various passages. This first principle provides the first step in our interpretive framework by ensuring all decisions fit within the mission of God.

Several foundational theological principles were given to aid in understanding this principle. First, the example of God revealing himself in his Son gives us a model of how we are to act toward others. All of the actions of the Son are for the purpose of glorifying the Father. Second, diversity in all of its various aspects is one of the primary means by which God reveals himself to his people. Third, following the Great Commission, we should work to move our congregations from practice to praxis such that our faith becomes evident and genuine in our lives. Finally, the New Covenant has shifted our relational approach such that love should be the core motivation. These principles should guide our thinking as we develop our philosophies of ministry, our policies and procedures, and our ministry practices.

Chapter 3 – Engaging Culture with our Christian Ethics

In this chapter I introduced the second principle that *our interpretation and decisions should lead to redemption in our current cultural setting.* Developing redemptive churches is not easy as healthy churches do not evolve naturally; they must be intentionally developed. At the heart of healthy churches are healthy relationships. This means that we need to help our people wrestle with sin and redemption in patient and loving ways and transfer this dynamic to our church cultures. Only then can we impact our broader cultures in the way Christ envisioned.

To accomplish this we need to first, understand the actual nature of sin and how redemption engages that sin. Jesus provides the primary model in that he regularly interacted with sinners with much patience and yet with intentional engagement. Second, rather than create an atmosphere of judgment, we need to help people understand their choices and the impact of their choices. But even then, we do not have the ability to convict, redeem, or transform. That is the unique role of the Holy Spirit. This is why patience is required. Third, the metaphors of priest and sacrifice help us understand how to create a redemptive culture in our churches. We are to sacrifice on behalf of our people as well as bless them. Finally, we need to learn how to let the Spirit play his role. We should not attempt to fulfill his role of conviction, redemption, or transformation. If our decisions detract from creating redemptive cultures, then we should check our interpretation.

Chapter 4 – Keeping the Line in the Sand

In this chapter I introduced the third principle that *our interpretations and decisions should be consistent with the freedoms established by the Bible.* Following John Stackhouse's proposal, I suggested that, since God was primarily interested in creating a healthy church to reflect his glory, this means that he is willing to forgo secondary objectives in order to further his primary purpose. Thus, I suggested that where the Bible draws a line in the sand, we should leave the line where it is drawn. Conversely, when the Bible makes allowances, we have freedom. Freedom to do whatever? Absolutely not. We must at this point go back to Principles #1 and #2.

This means that if we fail to exercise our freedom judiciously and go down the road of normalizing sin then we create additional theological challenges that limit our ability to fulfill God's mission. First, we have removed the need for redemption. The very nature of identifying sin is for the purpose of redemption rather than judgment. Second, we model for the world that morality does not matter. If morality does not matter, why go to church? Third, we send the underlying message that the Bible is neither important nor relevant. Our younger generations need to see integrity with the way we handle Scripture and redemptive challenges and provide life-giving answers when asked why we believe what we believe. It no longer works to say, "Because the Bible says so." Conversely, we should be careful not to default to the most conservative passage as this will lead us to even deeper problems. This will have the tendency of negating our freedom and even leading us to regress in our expression of Christian ethics.

It is of no redemptive help to either create unwelcome environments or environments that normalize sin. Where the Bible is consistent, so should we be. Conversely, where the Bible creates "doubleness," we should carefully work to create healthier and better redemptive approaches within our own cultural context. If our practices, rituals, traditions, and behaviors as a church do not lead to this result, we should check our interpretation.

Chapter 5 – Following the Movement of God in Biblical History

In this chapter I introduced the fourth principle *that our interpretation and decisions should be consistent with the theological development of the Bible as it unfolds.* If we understand God's incredible and loving redemptive engagement with culture for the purpose of restoration, then we can navigate how to interact with other cultures (including our own). Is the answer simply to bring them up to the current ethic taught in Scripture, or to gently and patiently move them to a better ethic in a slow and redeeming fashion? Here we proposed that wherever we find a cultural ethic that is lagging behind Scripture, we follow the pattern of God's graceful and patient engagement toward restoration. In contrast, we also proposed that where cultural redemption has occurred beyond the story of the Bible, leave the biblical passages in the "museum of redemption" rather than attempt to enculturate them into today's developed system of ethics so that we can marvel at how God worked in very challenging situations.

As discussed earlier in leaving the line in the sand, all that the Bible teaches about God and the character of God is absolutely true. It may be an emerging theology in that God reveals himself slowly over time, but all that is true of God remains true of God and has always been true of God. Conversely, in the areas of social and personal concerns, the Bible shows consistent development. This should not be surprising as this seems to be God's preferred way of engaging his people. And these transitions and growth did not happen *quickly*! But they did happen *steadily* as God revealed himself over time. Using Webb's model, we suggested that the larger story of redemption found in the Bible, especially as it relates to the story of Israel, is *itself* a model of creating healthy churches.

What this all means is that our interpretation and decisions should be consistent with the theological development of the Bible as it unfolds. Since the ethics of Scripture (as captured by the stories, applications, and commands) demonstrate development, the way we use Scripture in our various contexts should demonstrate similar sensitivity and patience to the complex issues with which we are faced.

Chapter 6 – Bringing the Kingdom into Our Present World

In this chapter I introduced the fifth principle that *our interpretation and decisions should bring the eschatological kingdom into our present world*, so that the surrounding culture can more clearly see God's mission being fulfilled. Since we have a different ethic, our love should motivate us as churches to move into the lives of our community at large. If we are to fully live out the Lord's prayer that the kingdom of God would come as it is in heaven, then we need to more fully grasp the principles behind kingdom living.

First, as our conversations and sermons about God become more life-giving, we increasingly become people who attract others to our beliefs (Titus 2:9–10). This means that we begin to wrestle with and understand our own congregations better and work to create safe spaces for them to wrestle with the Spirit and allow him to do his work. Second, it also means that we more fully grasp our responsibility and privilege of being a people set apart with a unique ethic to accomplish an incredible mission—the mission of God. Finally, when we balance our freedoms in Christ with our love for our cultures, we begin to look for and find ways to live in society in life-changing ways. As Christians we become more acutely aware of the tension between the present (now) and the hope of glory (not yet). This means we learn to be bold where we can be and conservative and sensitive where we need to be, all for the sake of mission. These are the reasons that all of our interpretations and decisions should be oriented toward bringing the kingdom of God into our present world.

Chapter 7 – Creating a Flourishing Faith Community

In this chapter I introduced the sixth principle that *our interpretation and decisions should lead to a flourishing community of faith.* In order to effectively bring the kingdom out to our broader culture, it is critical that we first take stock of our own internal organizational health. The health of our surrounding culture and our ability to genuinely share the love of Christ is dependent on our health as a church. There is no shortcut to this health. It begins with the individuals in our churches when they experience redemption in their own lives. As these experiences add up this creates a powerful and dynamic group of people who bring blessing to those they love.

Here we defined a flourishing church in terms of increasing coherency between our stated (confessional) beliefs and our lived out (actual) beliefs. As these two areas come together in integrity, genuine redemption and relational safety result. As we interpret Scripture and develop approaches to challenges, it is critical that we keep in front of us the responsibility of continuing to strive for flourishment. This is what will draw people to our churches, rather than push them away.

Using These Principles

So, how do we use these principles? Using the decision-making paradigm, I suggest the following.

119

Step 1 – Carefully work hard at clarifying the actual problem. This is the hardest part of the process. The work done here will directly impact how the process unfolds. Failure to accurately and clearly state the problem always leads to confusion, division, and failure to solve the underlying issue.

Step 2 – Ask your people what their natural instinct is once the problem is clear. The Holy Spirit *can be* trusted. This step will begin to put on the table those desires, aspirations, possible approaches and solutions, which will bless your church or organization.

Step 3 – Analyze, with your group, and clarify the theological principles that need to be addressed from the desires identified in step 2 in order to move toward clearly defined options.

Step 4 – Take the clearly defined options and apply them against the six principles (the framework of interpretation) in this book. If they pass all six, then you have freedom to proceed. If any of the proposed options do not meet all six criteria, take them off the table and remove them from the list.

Step 5 – Choose one of the options and implement it. Allow for mistakes to be made! Regularly review your decisions and see if adjustments need to be made as culture shifts around you.

Conclusion

A final word. Having used this approach in the classroom, my own church, Nepal, and Mozambique, I am continually blessed when I see the results. I often stand back in awe as the groups find very creative and inspiring solutions to problems that I would have no idea how to approach. In both Nepal and Mozambique, their cultural problems often are quite different than our own here... so much so that I find myself, at their enjoyment, scratching my head in figuring out how they got there and where to start in the decision-making and problem-solving process (see Appendix 1 for an example from Mozambique).

It is quite daunting to entrust a group of people to the leadership of the Holy Spirit. But when I have done this very thing and allowed this approach to unfold under his guidance, I am stunned and pleased at the possibilities that open up. Be bold. Do not be afraid of the Holy Spirit. Remember, we are allowed to make mistakes... and often do. You can trust the Holy Spirit to teach, guide, and lead. You should also be able to trust your leaders, most of whom have been tested through the trials of life. This lies behind the exhortation of Hebrews 13:7, "Remember your leaders, who spoke the word of God to you. Consider the outcome of their way of life and imitate their faith." They have made many mistakes, and yet their faith is real and their intuition trustworthy. As John reminds us, "You, dear children, are from God and have overcome them, because the one who is in you is greater than the one who is in the world" (1 John 4:4).

Appendix 1

MOZAMBIQUE: A TEST CASE

O n a recent trip to Mozambique I worked with 80 pastors at a conference sponsored and hosted by the Centro para o Desenvolvimento de Liderança (CDL) in Maputo, Mozambique. These pastors were from different parts of the country, different tribes, and different Christian traditions. After teaching through these principles, they had the opportunity to identify a problem and then develop options to be considered.

Step 1 – Identifying and clarifying the problem. In this part of the process we divided the group into smaller groups and asked them to select problems they faced in their churches in which they had little agreement or biblical guidance. They identified the following broad categories:

1. Sensuality in the church – a tendency to let emotionalism take precedence over and control the worship and teaching of the service.
2. Witchcraft in the church – the tendency of their members to "hedge their bets" against sickness, disease, fortune telling, etc. by contacting the local pastor, the local "witch doctor," and the local priest and asking for blessing and help from all three.

3. Handling cultural differences in the wedding ceremony – see below.

4. Alcoholism among the leadership of the church – a consistent pattern among the leaders to give in to alcoholism (with some drug use).

5. Child prostitution – this was a large area that encompassed childhood sexual abuse, sex trafficking, prostitution of children in order to derive additional revenues.

6. Tithing – a tendency on the part of many people who did not tithe for a variety of reasons including being too poor and lack of theological education.

7. False prophets and heresy – a consistent pattern of people rising up claiming to be prophets, but who delivered false prophecies and heresies to the congregation.

After they all discussed it in their groups and voted, they unanimously selected #3 – the handling of cultural differences in the wedding ceremony. After thoroughly discussing this area and all the many facets involved, they narrowed it down to the problem related to invoking the spirits of the dead family patriarchs.

As part of the process of engagement leading up to the ceremony, the groom must approach the matriarch of the family who is not the mother and ask for blessing from the bride's family. The matriarch would then consult the spirits of the dead patriarchs to discern what they would require in order to bestow a blessing on the wedding ceremony and the marriage. They would typically not divulge the requirement until the day before the ceremony and would commonly ask for one year's salary to be paid to the bride's family. The pastors recognized that this was a satanic problem that often led to worship of ancestors and assigning authority to the dead spirits.

The problem lay in the ongoing relationship between the families. If the groom refused to honor the requirements for the blessing, he would have to call off the wedding and face embarrassment and possible cultural persecution or continue with the ceremony thus incurring a lifetime of cursing by the bride's family. It was not a simple matter of refusing based on biblical grounds. The impact was long-lasting no matter which way the groom decided. As most grooms could not afford a year's salary, this placed an undue heavy burden on the groom, while simultaneously placing the bride in a challenging position between both families. Additionally, the pastors were appropriately concerned with the impact on the local congregation who observed the entire process.

Step 2 – Identifying the informed collective intuition. Once the problem was clear and everyone agreed on the particulars of the problem, I placed them back in their groups to identify desires and possible solutions. As they had difficulty identifying any clear biblical path to resolution, their key desires surfaced along several lines:

1. They desired to have the elders sit with the bride's family and attempt to either transform their thinking or persuade them to negotiate and accept a lesser offer.
2. They desired to work with the bride to accept her rejection or cursing, if necessary, for the sake of biblical truth in that they could not ask her to accept the authority of the dead spirits.
3. They desired to have the family of the bride participate in the wedding ceremony in an attempt to have them lessen the requirement as they experienced the joy of the ceremony.
4. They desired to have the bride's family attend church in genuine hopes for their conversion and later lessening of the burden placed on the groom.

All of these practices had been tried on several occasions by each of the pastors with very little success. They felt trapped in that they were caught between their biblical training related to having nothing to do with dead spirits and risking the curses of the bride's family for the remainder of the marriage and the resulting and ongoing damage of those curses in the marriage relationship.

Step 3 – Surfacing the theological principles that needed addressing in order to inform their desires. As part of the discussion, they surfaced a variety of theological principles that needed addressing. Among the key principles and questions that the groups identified and agreed upon were the following:

1. What is the biblical definition of marriage and the role it plays in reflecting God's love for their surrounding culture?
2. What is the function of communication and how does it work in situations like this?
3. What does it mean to honor parents, even if they do not know the Lord or agree with the church?
4. What is meant by holiness in marriage, within families, and between families. Additionally, what was the impact of taking a "holy" or "unholy" approach on their congregations?
5. What is meant by family unity?
6. What does it mean to obey God in this situation?
7. What role does accommodation and compromise play in this situation?

There were several other theological principles that we worked through, but these are sufficient to illustrate how the paradigm works. At this point I had them point to biblical stories and teachings that provided insight into each of the theological principles. It soon became apparent that the last question of accommodation and compromise rose to the surface as the most important principle in the discussion. This is because they were familiar with the other theological principles but had never seriously considered compromise as a legitimate option.

As they narrowed down the discussion to possible compromise, they reflected on how God had consistently compromised throughout history for the sake of the gospel. What if that was a possibility in this case? As they worked in their groups, they identified several areas of identifiable compromise beyond what I discussed earlier in chapter 5. For example, they surfaced Matthew 22:21 and Jesus' teaching on giving to Caesar what belonged to him.[250] Since the Roman Empire was funding numerous programs that were clearly outside of God's desires for his people, it was an act of compromise to give to Caesar (i.e. the Roman government) his due. They reasoned that Christ felt that being good citizens and representing the kingdom was more important than standing their ground. They argued that Acts 16 and the story of the Philippian jailer was another example. When he asked what he must do to be saved, Paul and Silas responded with "Believe!" They said nothing about the idols and gods that the jailer and his family probably worshipped... that came later.

As a result of this step we filled the whiteboards with many biblical stories and teachings that further "filled in" their idea of what was possible. I asked them what would have happened had we gone straight from the problem to the Bible and skipped the process? In their estimation, how many of these biblical passages would they have considered? Their combined intuition said about 10-20%. Taking them through the process led them deeper into the further reaches of Scripture than they would have otherwise considered.

Step 4 – Developing and testing the options against the six principles. At this point we went back to the desires expressed in step 2 and reformulated them into options for them to consider. We then applied the six principles to their options and one surfaced that met all six criteria and they unanimously approved.

Their new approach was to take the groom and one elder to the bride's family and explain their Christian faith and values first to see if the Holy Spirit was at work in the bride's family. If it was clear that he had not yet opened their hearts, they would then work to negotiate a lesser settlement. If that did not work, then the church, partnering with the groom, and with the bride's family aware, would pay the settlement amount to illustrate to the bride's family that the church stood with the married couple, both in their marriage and in their relationship with the bride's family. They felt this was an appropriate place to compromise some level of their faith for the sake of the gospel. Their action would also demonstrate to their congregations that they stood in solidarity with each member of the congregation.

A final word about this process. It was meaningful to me that the problem they eventually chose was one in which I had no previous experience nor idea how to advise. I thoroughly enjoyed the process over several days of watching them discuss and debate and slowly come together to form a strategy that went "beyond" Scripture and in which they all were confident. They were confident that their final decision gave them concrete guidance where the Bible was unclear, and yet was a decision that honored the Lord, their traditions, the people involved in the challenge, their congregations, and their own consciences.

Endnotes

1   The science and art of biblical interpretation.

2   Miroslav Volf, *Captive to the Word of God: Engaging the Scriptures for Contemporary Theological Reflection* (Grand Rapids, MI: Eerdmans, 2010), 15–40. Volf goes further and appropriately states concerning the Bible, "its interpretation is best undertaken against the backdrop of its multiple settings: economic, cultural, political, etc... The Bible is therefore appropriately read as a narration of happenings, with an aim to understand what took place then and there and how what took place then and there was understood. A theological reading will do more than that; it will also attend to what bearing these past happenings have on what needs to happen here and now. It should not do less." Ibid., 16.

3   Bernard L. Ramm, *Protestant Biblical Interpretation: A Textbook of Hermeneutics*, 3rd rev. ed. (Grand Rapids, MI: Baker, 1970), 1. As a very young student in college, I still remember the excitement I felt when I first began reading Ramm's textbook. To this day, I still feel the thrill of doing the hard work to grasp the interpretation and meaning of a text and then communicating it to others in life-changing ways.

4   Ibid., 186–89.

5   To be fair, Ramm's intention was to bring the focus in Protestant hermeneutics back to a more centralized orthodox position. In the preface to his original work Wilber Smith claims, "Probably in no department of Biblical or theological study has there been such a lack of worthwhile literature in the twentieth century as in the field of Biblical hermeneutics." He goes on to call the literature produced in the twentieth century "trivial, wretchedly written, fragmentary works, without exact scholarship and incapable of making real contributions to this study." Ibid., xv–xvi.

6   The field is much too large to list all of the works and is constantly expanding. The following excellent works are representative. Craig G. Bartholomew, *Introducing Biblical Hermeneutics: A Comprehensive Framework for Hearing God in Scripture* (Grand Rapids, MI: Baker, 2015); Craig A. Carter, *Interpreting Scripture with the Great Tradition: Recovering the Genius of Premodern Exegesis* (Grand Rapids, MI: Baker Academic, 2018); Jason S. DeRouchie, *How to Understand and Apply the Old Testament: Twelve Steps from Exegesis to Theology* (Phillipsburg,

NJ: P&R Publishing, 2017); J. Scott Duvall and J. Daniel Hays, *Grasping God's Word: A Hands-on Approach to Reading, Interpreting, and Applying the Bible*, 3rd ed. (Grand Rapids, MI: Zondervan, 2012); Michael J. Gorman, ed. *Scripture and Its Interpretation: A Global, Ecumenical Introduction to the Bible* (Grand Rapids, MI: Baker, 2017); Joel B. Green, *Practicing Theological Interpretation: Engaging Biblical Texts for Faith and Formation* (Grand Rapids, MI: Baker, 2012); Craig S. Keener, *Spirit Hermeneutics: Reading Scripture in Light of Pentecost* (Grand Rapids, MI: Eerdmans, 2016); William W. Klein, Craig L. Blomberg, and Robert L. Hubbard, *Introduction to Biblical Interpretation*, 3rd ed. (Grand Rapids, MI: Zondervan, 2017); Grant R. Osborne, *The Hermeneutical Spiral: A Comprehensive Introduction to Biblical Interpretation*, Rev. and expanded, 2nd ed. (Downers Grove, IL: InterVarsity, 2006); Volf, *Captive*; William J. Webb, *Slaves, Women & Homosexuals: Exploring the Hermeneutics of Cultural Analysis* (Downers Grove, IL: InterVarsity, 2001); N. T. Wright, *Scripture and the Authority of God*, 2nd rev. and expanded ed. (London: SPCK, 2013).

7   David F. Wells, *No Place for Truth, or, Whatever Happened to Evangelical Theology?* (Grand Rapids, MI: Eerdmans, 1993), 218–57. In his evaluation of Wells, Alister McGrath argued that "there is a widespread consensus within evangelicalism that Wells had identified a real and worrying trend within the movement, even if his particular presentation of these defects is perhaps somewhat overstated." Alister E. McGrath, *A Passion for Truth: The Intellectual Coherence of Evangelicalism* (Downers Grove, IL: InterVarsity, 1996), 12.

8   John G. Stackhouse, "Preface," in *Evangelical Futures: A Conversation on Theological Methoc*, ed. John G. Stackhouse, (Downers Grove, IL: InterVarsity, 1996), 9.

9   I am indebted to the Scripture and Hermeneutics Seminar (Institute for Biblical Research). Many of their principles have guided me in this study. Their framework is published in Craig G. Bartholomew and Heath A. Thomas, eds., *A Manifesto for Theological Interpretation* (Grand Rapids, MI: Baker, 2016).

10   Charles H. Kraft, *Christianity in Culture: A Study in Dynamic Biblical Theologizing in Cross Cultural Perspective*, 2nd ed. (Maryknoll, NY: Orbis, 2005), 13.

11   Dean E. Flemming, *Contextualization in the New Testament: Patterns for Theology and Mission* (Downers Grove, IL: InterVarsity, 2005), 14.

12   Interestingly, Grant Osborne, when moving toward principles of application, actually titles his chapter "Homiletics I: Contextualization." Osborne, *Hermeneutical Spiral*, 410. This reveals his tendency to place the burden on effective application within the context of preaching. While I do not disagree, as a pastor I have learned that the process of decision-making moves far beyond the boundaries of preaching.

13   With the use of the phrase "easily accessible" I am referring to the ease and ability of pastors and leaders to access and utilize clear principles on a day-to-day basis. The term is not meant to be pejorative as I am deeply grateful for each of these

works and the role they have played in shaping my own ministry and theology. However, pastors and leaders must make decisions on a day-to-day basis and need easier models to guide them as they lead and shepherd.

14   I am grateful for my colleague, Don Payne, at Denver Seminary and the more than 10 years of discussion in this area. We co-teach FC1101 – Biblical and Theological Reflection on the Practice of Ministry in the Denver Seminary Doctor of Ministry program where we flesh out this model in great detail.

15   Anyone who has taught doctoral students for any length of time recognizes this problem in the development of theses and dissertations. A key part of their education is learning to trim down the impossibly broad topic to a topic that can be managed.

16   This is part of the critique leveled by Christian Smith, *The Bible Made Impossible: Why Biblicism Is Not a Truly Evangelical Reading of Scripture* (Grand Rapids, MI: Brazos, 2011, 2012).

17   For a discussion on the role of the church, see Robby Holt and Aubrey Spears, "The Ecclesia as the Primary Context for the Reception of the Bible," in *A Manifesto for Theological Interpretation*, ed. Craig G. Bartholomew and Heath A. Thomas, (Grand Rapids, MI: Baker, 2016). I have applied their thoughts to the need to properly identify the problem and begin to surface possible solutions.

18   For an example and analysis of how informed intuition works, see the fascinating book by Malcolm Gladwell, *Blink: The Power of Thinking without Thinking* (New York: Little, Brown and Co., 2005). In this delightful book, Gladwell looks at many areas of society and questions how people, in the blink of an eye, can make astute observations and decisions about challenges facing them. He concludes that it is related to the degree to which a person grows in their understanding of a particular area. The more they study or are exposed to information in a particular area, the more informed (and formed) their intuition becomes. As Christians, we have the Holy Spirit constantly guiding, informing, and shaping us. I am grateful for my elders whose informed intuition has been shaped through the trials of life and have come out faithful in all areas of life.

19   It does not matter the order of steps #3 and #4. I put #3 first as this part of the discussion will often generate ideas needed in #4. However, if #4 has already been proposed and ideas are on the table, it is appropriate to ask the question of #3 to ensure integrity with Scripture. Remember, we are addressing situations where the Bible may not be clear. If the Bible is clear, then we must follow it. More on this later in the study.

20   I am using his language to capture an image of the questions that need to be asked when applying Scripture to present day issues. He uses the concept of a framework more to inform his readings of the biblical texts. "As I read Scripture, I am guided by an integrated set of convictions about the Bible and its interpretation." Volf, *Captive*, 15. While I certainly agree and have my own "set of convictions," I have expanded his idea into the realm of interpretation and decision-making.

Chapter 1

21   Duvall and Hays, *Grasping*, 238.

22   Klein et al., *Interpretation*, 604.

23   An excellent example of this are the challenges of how to help the poor without hurting them. There are many books written on this topic. For more recent discussions in this area see Brian Fikkert and Kelly M. Kapic, *Becoming Whole: Why the Opposite of Poverty Isn't the American Dream* (Chicago, IL: Moody, 2019); Steve Corbett and Brian Fikkert, *When Helping Hurts: How to Alleviate Poverty without Hurting the Poor and Yourself* (Chicago, IL: Moody, 2009); Marvin N. Olasky, *The Tragedy of American Compassion* (Wheaton, IL: Crossway, 1992); Robert D. Lupton, *Toxic Charity: How Churches and Charities Hurt Those They Help (and How to Reverse It)* (New York, NY: Harper, 2011).

24   For the purposes of this study, I am assuming all of the hermeneutical and exegetical work has been done to accurately work through and identify the interpretation of any given text. As Roy Zuck reminds us, "The role of the Spirit in interpretation is no substitute for diligent study." Roy B Zuck, "The Role of the Holy Spirit in Hermeneutics," *Bibliotheca Sacra* 141, no. 562 (1984): 125.

25   For an excellent overview of the complexities involved, see Osborne, *Hermeneutical Spiral*, 465–521.

26   Ibid., 520.

27   I am defining biblicism, not as one who holds to a high view of Scripture and seeks to obey it, but as one who uses only the Bible for their source of knowledge, blindly holding to the Bible to guide them through every situation and inform them on every issue.

28   Volf, *Captive*, 15–40. As explained in the Introduction, I am using his language to capture an image of the questions that need to be asked when applying Scripture to present day issues. He uses the concept of a framework to inform his readings of the biblical texts. While I certainly agree and have my own "set of convictions," I have expanded his idea into the realm of interpretation and decision-making.

29   Green, *Practicing*, 71–80.

30   Kevin J. Vanhoozer et al., eds., *Dictionary for Theological Interpretation of the Bible* (London, England and Grand Rapids, MI: Society for Promoting Christian Knowledge and Baker Academic, 2005), 703.

31   Green, *Practicing*, 72.

32   Ibid., 74.

33   Heath A. Thomas, "The Telos (Goal) of Theological Interpretation," in *A Manifesto for Theological Interpretation*, ed. Craig G. Bartholomew and Heath A. Thomas, (Grand Rapids, MI: Baker, 2016), 205.

34 I'm thinking at this point of the shifting cultural milieu of the United States of America although I am confident other cultures have their own unique challenges.

35 Paul G. Hiebert, *Anthropological Insights for Missionaries* (Grand Rapids, MI: Baker, 1985), 30.

36 I believe more work needs to be done to evaluate the New Testament through the lens of ethnic diversity. Romans is written to Italians, Titus is written to Crete (a Mediterranean island culture), and so on. Much evangelical training is appropriately focused on identifying the cohesive elements of Scripture. When looked at through the lens of ethnic diversity, things look differently. The differences that surface are intriguing and demonstrate that even the New Testament authors allowed for some freedom and variety in application. More on this later.

37 It would be intriguing, for example, to compare how a Baptist church in Fairview, Oklahoma would respond to the question of a different sexual orientation in the same way as my church in Dillon, Colorado where only 7% of the county self-identify as Protestant Christians and where the many denominations present in the church represent differing views on this topic.

38 Lesslie Newbigin, *The Gospel in a Pluralist Society* (Grand Rapids, MI: Eerdmans, 1989), 184.

39 In this section I am following the general outline proposed by the Scripture and Hermeneutics Seminar in Bartholomew and Thomas, eds., *A Manifesto for Theological Interpretation*, 1–25. I am summarizing the principles here. A fuller discussion of each of these principles is found in the various chapters of the book.

40 Carter states, "we should read the Bible as a unity centered on Jesus Christ... The bottom line, the nonnegotiable foundation of the Great Tradition, is the firm conviction that the Bible is a unified book." Carter, *Interpreting*, 130.

41 Baruch A. Levine, *Numbers 21–36: A New Translation with Introduction and Commentary*, ed. William Foxwell Albright and David Noel Freedman, Anchor Bible (New York: Doubleday, 2000), 322.

42 Ibid., 341.

43 Jacob Milgrom, *Numbers: The Traditional Hebrew Text with the New JPS Translation*, ed. Nahum M. Sarna, JPS Torah Commentary (Philadelphia and New York: Jewish Publication Society, 1990), 232.

44 R. Dennis Cole, *Numbers*, ed. E. Ray Clendenen, New American Commentary, vol. 3B (Nashville, TN: Broadman & Holman, 2000), 464-66. He argues that the very structure of the presentation contributes to our understanding of the development of casuistic legislation in Israelite history. Thus, it becomes precedent setting in its own right.

45 Ibid., 464. "It seems best to face the fact that Num 27:1–11 is about the rights of daughters" in Philip J. Budd, *Numbers*, ed. David A. Hubbard, Glenn W. Barker, and John D. W. Watts, Word Biblical Commentary, vol. 5 (Waco, TX: Word,

1984), 301. "The daughters of Zelophehad consequently sought a new ruling that would allow daughters to inherit" in Levine, *Numbers 21–36*, 345.

46　For a fascinating discussion on several other unusual features in this text, see Ralph W. Klein, *2 Chronicles: A Commentary*, ed. Paul D. Hanson, Hermeneia—a Critical and Historical Commentary on the Bible (Minneapolis, MN: Fortress, 2012), 427–42. Something similar had happened in Moses' time when the people had not been purified because they had touched a corpse. As a result, he postponed the Passover one month with the permission of the Lord (Num 9:6–13).

47　Jacob Martin Myers, *II Chronicles*, ed. William Foxwell Albright and David Noel Freedman, Anchor Bible, (Garden City, NY: Doubleday, 1965), 177. The biblical reference formatting has been updated to provide consistency.

48　Eckhard J. Schnabel, *Acts*, ed. Clinton E. Arnold, Zondervan Exegetical Commentary on the New Testament, vol. 5 (Grand Rapids, MI: Zondervan, 2012), 473. The outline of this section follows Schnabel's commentary.

49　For an accessible explanation, see Jacob Milgrom, *Leviticus: A Book of Ritual and Ethics*, Continental Commentary (Minneapolis, MN: Fortress, 2004), 102–21.

50　Schnabel, *Acts*, 491.

51　Ibid., 632. Italics mine.

52　For a summary and discussion of the arguments, see ibid., 644–45.

53　I am grateful to David Instone-Brewer for our discussions while at Tyndale House on this passage, the details of what the actual charge was, and how this might benefit my argument in this study. The story is also found in Mark 2:23–28 and Luke 6:1–11 with some variations not treated here.

54　The Sabbath laws and Rabbinic tradition are quite complex. For the purposes of this study, the core rebuttal of Jesus serves to illustrate his principles regarding the law.

55　Craig S. Keener, *The Gospel of Matthew: A Socio-Rhetorical Commentary* (Grand Rapids, MI and Cambridge, United Kingdom: Eerdmans, 2009), 355.

56　Ibid., 354.

57　Ibid., 353–56.

58　David J. Rudolph, *A Jew to the Jews: Jewish Contours of Pauline Flexibility in 1 Corinthians 9:19–23*, ed. Jörg Frey, Wissenschaftliche Untersuchungen Zum Neuen Testament 2 Reihe, vol. 304 (Tübingen: Mohr Siebeck, 2011), 181. This work is a technical but fascinating study in how Jesus influenced Paul in what Rudolph calls "Jesus' rule of adoption." We do not consider Paul in the present study, but Rudolph brings other examples of Paul's ministry to the table for consideration.

59　Ibid., 181–82.

60   Grant R. Osborne, *Matthew*, ed. Clinton E. Arnold, Zondervan Exegetical Commentary on the New Testament (Grand Rapids, MI: Zondervan, 2010), 452–53.

61   Sandra L. Richter, *The Epic of Eden: A Christian Entry into the Old Testament* (Downers Grove, IL: IVP Academic, 2008), 75.

62   Gary V. Smith, *Hosea, Amos, Micah*, ed. Terry Muck, NIV Application Commentary (Grand Rapids, MI: Zondervan, 2001), 112.

63   D. A. Baer and R. P. Gordon, "חסד," in *New International Dictionary of Old Testament Theology and Exegesis*, ed. Willem A. VanGemeren, (Grand Rapids, MI: Zondervan, 1996), vol. 2, 211.

64   Osborne, *Matthew*, 454.

65   Keener, *Matthew*, 355.

Chapter 2

66   Christopher J. H. Wright, *The Mission of God: Unlocking the Bible's Grand Narrative* (Downers Grove, IL: InterVarsity, 2006), 33.

67   Andreas J. Köstenberger and Peter Thomas O'Brien, *Salvation to the Ends of the Earth: A Biblical Theology of Mission*, ed. D. A. Carson, New Studies in Biblical Theology (Leicester, England and Downers Grove, IL: Apollos and InterVarsity, 2001), 20.

68   Flemming, *Contextualization*, 318.

69   Wright, *Mission of God*, 22–23.

70   Kraft, *Culture*, 118–21.

71   Ibid., 118.

72   Ibid., 119.

73   Richard Bauckham, *Bible and Mission: Christian Witness in a Postmodern World* (Grand Rapids, MI: Baker Academic, 2003), 8–9.

74   "The table of nations, unique in world literature, paints a basically positive, or at least neutral, picture of the relationships between the nations… Were that the end of the story, the reader would conclude that the sons of Noah lived in brotherly concord, fulfilling God's command to fill the earth and subdue it. The very much shorter tower of Babel story corrects this interpretation." Gordon J. Wenham, *Genesis 1–15*, ed. David A. Hubbard, Glenn W. Barker, and John D. W. Watts, Word Biblical Commentary, vol. 1 (Nashville, TN: Thomas Nelson, 1987), 242. This is ultimately corrected in the wonderful picture of persons from every tribe and language and people and nation standing before God singing his new song (Rev 5:9–10). Additionally, Rev 5:10 is a clear reference back to Sinai where God's intentions are made clear that he desires a kingdom of priests (Exod 19:3–6). Peter understands that this has been accomplished among the nations (1 Pet 1:1; 2:9–10). In between lies the mission of God.

75 Ibid., 245.

76 Wright, *Mission of God*, 65.

77 Craig L. Blomberg, *1 Corinthians*, ed. Terry Muck, NIV Application Commentary (Grand Rapids, MI: Zondervan, 1994), 186. Italics mine.

78 My experience has amply demonstrated to me that, if a pastor is going to be unfaithful, most evangelical churches secretly hope it is in a heterosexual relationship rather than a homosexual relationship. We have become more comfortable with thinking through and managing one over the other even though theologically we can demonstrate them both to be biblically defined as sin of adultery.

79 For a helpful introduction to this question, see N. T. Wright, *Scripture and the Authority of God: How to Read the Bible Today*, Rev. and exp. ed. (United Kingdom: Society for Promoting Christian Knowledge, 2011; reprint, HarperCollins 2013).

80 Galatians 5:1 is helpful at this point, "It is for freedom that Christ has set us free." More on this in chapter 3.

81 Wright, *Scripture*, 31.

82 I understand that obeying the Lord's commands does bring joy, but that is not how modern culture defines happiness.

83 In constructing a kingdom hermeneutic, Bauckham argues that it is necessary how "the Bible as a whole tells a story, in some sense a single story, an overall narrative encompassing, of course, many other stories and including many forms of non-narrative literature within it, but constituting in its overall direction a metanarrative, a narrative about the whole of reality." Bauckham, *Mission*, 12.

84 For an excellent, although technical, work on this topic see Ellen T. Charry, *By the Renewing of Your Minds: The Pastoral Function of Christian Doctrine* (New York, NY and Oxford, England: Oxford University, 1997).

85 Wright, *Mission of God*, 23.

86 Gerald Bray, *God Is Love: A Biblical and Systematic Theology* (Wheaton, IL: Crossway, 2012), 17.

87 Ibid., 107.

88 This is not to say that grace and compassion can be overlooked. More on this later.

89 Perhaps this reflects how we, as pastors, have taught our congregations. It strikes me that the discussion of the law is more of an academic discussion for most Christians as most have never actually read it. When one actually reads the law, it immediately becomes clear that the law was not the problem. Perhaps this is why Paul could "claim" that as for righteousness based on the law, he was faultless (Phil 3:6).

90 John N. Oswalt, *Called to Be Holy: A Biblical Perspective* (Anderson, IN: Francis Asbury, 1999), 89.

91 Darrell L. Bock, *Luke*, ed. Robert W. Yarbrough and Robert H. Stein, 2 vols., Baker Exegetical Commentary on the New Testament (Grand Rapids: Baker,

1994–96), 1:406. He goes further and argues that the image of freedom for the captives "includes release from sin and spiritual captivity." Ibid., 1:409.

92 "Jesus has demonstrated his love for his own (13:1ff.), declared his love for them and commanded them to love one another (13:34–35); now for the first time in the Fourth Gospel he speaks of their love for him. The conditional is third class: Jesus neither assumes that his followers love him, nor assumes that they do not, even for the sake of the argument, but projects a condition and stipulates its entailment: they *will obey* (the future, not the imperative, is the correct reading) what he commands." D. A. Carson, *The Gospel According to John*, ed. D. A. Carson, Pillar New Testament Commentary (Leicester, England and Grand Rapids, MI: Apollos and Eerdmans, 1991), 498.

93 Ibid., 503.

Chapter 3

94 Wells, *No Place*, 98. With respect, Wells is addressing the "collapse" of theology in both the church and the academy. I do believe he has correctly surfaced an issue, but it may have many more aspects than he treats in his argument.

95 This principle helps understand the growing challenges around student ministries. The student is with their parents and schoolteachers over a hundred hours each week. It is unrealistic to expect a youth pastor to overcome these ingrained values by spending 2–4 hours each week with the students. The youth pastor can only work effectively within the structure created by the parents. If sports and other activities are more important than church attendance, the youth pastor has very little ability to overcome these parent-driven values. In other words, the youth pastor can only work with whatever values the parents have created in their families.

96 For a person in a failed marriage, simply finding improvement in the next marriage may feel better, but that does not mean they have experienced the delightful feelings that come with a good first marriage.

97 All are essential. A good marriage needs to be experienced before the principles of Scripture can be affectively understood. In contrast, very few Christians "feel" that they want to be generous in their financial giving. They must practice giving *before* they begin to learn how much joy can be derived by blessing others.

98 Keener, *Spirit Hermeneutics*, 25.

99 I would also suggest that many church discipline strategies reveal an inadequate view of sin as well. More on that later.

100 E. A. Martens, "Sin, Guilt," in *Dictionary of the Old Testament: Pentateuch*, ed. T. Desmond Alexander and David W. Baker, (Downers Grove, IL and Leicester, England: InterVarsity, 2003), 765. This is an excellent article to capture the many nuances of this complex subject.

101 Michael F. Bird, *Evangelical Theology: A Biblical and Systematic Introduction* (Grand Rapids, MI: Zondervan, 2013), 667.

102 Cornelius Plantinga, *Not the Way It's Supposed to Be: A Breviary of Sin* (Grand Rapids, MI and Leicester, England: Eerdmans and Apollos, 1995), 13–14. Italics mine.

103 P. A. Barker, "Rest, Peace," in *Dictionary of the Old Testament: Pentateuch*, ed. T. Desmond Alexander and David W. Baker, (Downers Grove, IL and Leicester, England: InterVarsity, 2003), 690.

104 It is worth asking whether or not we have raised sin to the level of being an idol in itself. When our view of sin leads to judgmental attitudes in the church and strategies that marginalize those in sin, I would argue that this deviates from the relational pattern of Jesus himself, is unhealthy, and may constitute an idolizing of sin.

105 "Not only is Jesus the divine image, but also he is the head of the new humanity destined to be formed according to that image in fulfillment of *God's intent for humankind from the beginning*." Stanley J. Grenz, *The Social God and the Relational Self: A Trinitarian Theology of the Imago Dei*, Matrix of Christian Theology (Louisville, KY: Westminster John Knox, 2001), 224. Italics mine.

106 John Frederic Kilner, *Dignity and Destiny: Humanity in the Image of God* (Grand Rapids, MI: Eerdmans, 2015), 92.

107 In one sense, the nature of the deception of sin is that we don't know what we don't know. A failed marriage might find more happiness and relief in a second marriage. However, those of us with good marriages naturally understand that additional marriages will struggle greatly to enjoy the richness and benefits of a good marriage done well the first time.

108 Elmer A. Martens, *God's Design: A Focus on Old Testament Theology*, 3rd ed. (N. Richland Hills, TX: BIBAL Press, 1998), 15.

109 Ibid., 10–11.

110 Richter, *Eden*, 40.

111 Wright, *Mission of God*, 266.

112 Ibid., 267.

113 Frederic W. Bush, *Ruth, Esther*, ed. David A. Hubbard, Glenn W. Barker, and John D. W. Watts, Word Biblical Commentary, vol. 9 (Dallas: Word books, 1996), 52.

114 The verb form of this word is what occurs in Exod 6:6 when God says that he will *redeem* Israel.

115 Wright, *Mission of God*, 266.

116 Robert L. Hubbard, *The Book of Ruth*, ed. R. K. Harrison, New International Commentary on the Old Testament (Grand Rapids, MI: Eerdmans, 1988), 65.

117 R. K. Duke, "Priests, Priesthood," in *Dictionary of the Old Testament: Pentateuch*, ed. T. Desmond Alexander and David W. Baker, (Downers Grove, IL and Leicester, England: InterVarsity, 2003), 650.

118 Wright, *Mission of God*, 330–31.

119 Ibid., 330.

120 Milgrom, *Leviticus*, 260.

121 Karen H. Jobes, *1 Peter*, ed. Robert W. Yarbrough and Robert H. Stein, Baker Exegetical Commentary on the New Testament (Grand Rapids, MI: Baker, 2005), 160–61.

122 I have written on this in more detail in James M. Howard, *Paul, the Community, and Progressive Sanctification: An Exploration into Community-Based Transformation within Pauline Theology*, ed. Hemchand Gossai, Studies in Biblical Literature, vol. 90 (New York: Peter Lang, 2007).

123 Averbeck has argued that the complex details involved in understanding the sacrificial system have made them a subject of *relatively little interest* to both scholars and Christians. The primary purpose of the sacrificial system was to provide a means of approaching the Lord in *his* location. Since Paul and Peter both used this metaphor, this makes it even more stunning that this area is largely overlooked in defining and creating redemptive environments. R. E. Averbeck, "Sacrifices and Offerings," in *Dictionary of the Old Testament: Pentateuch*, ed. T. Desmond Alexander and David W. Baker, (Downers Grove, IL and Leicester, England: InterVarsity, 2003), 706–07. Further, Watts begins his article on sacrifice with an astute observation. "The language of sacrifice pervades our contemporary rhetoric of politics, religion, and popular culture. References to sacrifice and depictions of sacrifice can be found in music lyrics, movies, political speeches, and news stories about sports, economics, and biomedical research. It is, of course, ubiquitous in the rhetoric of war." James W. Watts, "The Rhetoric of Sacrifice," in *Ritual and Metaphor: Sacrifice in the Bible*, ed. Christian Eberhart, Society of Biblical Literature Resources for Biblical Study, (Atlanta, GA: Society of Biblical Literature, 2011), vol. 68, 3. This helps explain Averbeck's statement about their being *relatively little interest*.

124 Schreiner has appropriately argued that the adjective "living" is one of three adjectives describing sacrifice. This passage is better understood in terms of offerings sacrifices which are alive, holy, and pleasing. In other words, "the word 'living' denotes the spiritual state of believers. They are now 'alive to God in Christ Jesus' (Rom. 6:11, 13; 8:13)." Thomas R. Schreiner, *Romans*, ed. Robert W. Yarbrough and Joshua W. Jipp, 2nd ed., Baker Exegetical Commentary on the New Testament (Grand Rapids: Baker Publishing Group, 2018), 626.

125 Jobes, *1 Peter*, 160.

126 A review of any technical commentary will give you the range of meaning of this term.

127 I am following Borchert's argument throughout. For a fuller description see Gerald L. Borchert, *John 12–21*, ed. E. Ray Clendenen, New American Commentary, vol. 25B (Nashville, TN: Broadman & Holman, 2002), 165–71.

128 Ibid., 166.

129 Ibid., 169.

130 Keener, *Matthew*, 454.

131 Osborne, *Matthew*, 687.

132 David L. Turner, *Matthew*, ed. Robert W. Yarbrough and Robert H. Stein, Baker Exegetical Commentary on the New Testament (Grand Rapids, MI: Baker Academic, 2008), 445.

133 The very words used in Peter's denials and oath are the very words used in Jesus' teachings.

134 Even Jesus' final statement to Judas might reveal some of this compassion (Matt 26:50). This verse is notoriously difficult to translate. With the use of "friend," I agree with Osborne, "Even knowing that Judas was there to 'hand him over' to his enemies, Jesus still shows acceptance and love for the man." Osborne, *Matthew*, 983.

Chapter 4

135 Thomas R. Schreiner, *Galatians*, ed. Clinton E. Arnold, Zondervan Exegetical Commentary on the New Testament (Grand Rapids, MI: Zondervan, 2010), 307.

136 Timothy George, *Galatians*, ed. E. Ray Clendenen and David S. Dockery, New American Commentary, vol. 30 (Nashville, TN: B&H, 1994), 351–52.

137 Robert Jewett and Roy D. Kotansky, *Romans: A Commentary*, ed. Eldon Jay Epp, Hermeneia—a Critical and Historical Commentary on the Bible (Minneapolis, MN: Fortress, 2007), 416.

138 George, *Galatians*, 376.

139 Mariam J. Kamell, "Life in the Spirit and Life in Wisdom," in *Galatians and Christian Theology: Justification, the Gospel, and Ethics in Paul's Letter*, ed. Mark W. Elliott et al., (Grand Rapids, MI: Baker, 2014), 355. Italics hers.

140 Bauckham further argues, "Liberation worthy of the name requires people who have been freed to live for others." Richard Bauckham, *God and the Crisis of Freedom: Biblical and Contemporary Perspectives* (Louisville, KY: Westminster John Knox Press, 2002), 25.

141 Scot McKnight, *Galatians*, ed. Terry Muck, NIV Application Commentary (Grand Rapids, MI: Zondervan, 1995), 271.

142 Ibid., 273. Italics mine.

143 Ibid.

144 Keener, *Spirit Hermeneutics*, 32. Italics mine. I was taught in seminary that it is wrong to bore people with the Word of God, and yet, I am continually amazed when I sit in a sermon or lecture and am bored, simply by hearing what I expect to hear. I am comforted that it is not because of my professional training, as many have expressed to me the same experience. Like the discussions in theology, when we are in the Word, it should be life-giving.

145 Schreiner, *Romans*, 723.

146 Keener, *Spirit Hermeneutics*, 21–38. Keener's chapter on experience is worth reading as he brings his academic and life experiences both into the discussion.

147 Ibid., 32.

148 Ibid., 34–35. "When those schooled in Scripture criticized the faith of a man who based his faith on his experience, he could only respond with, 'Once I was blind, but now I see,' and deconstruct the inconsistency of their arguments (John 9:25, 31–33)."

149 Bartholomew, *Hermeneutics*, 410.

150 John G. Stackhouse, *Finally Feminist: A Pragmatic Christian Understanding of Gender*, ed. Craig A. Evans and Lee Martin McDonald, Acadia Studies in Bible and Theology (Grand Rapids, MI: Baker, 2005). He uses his paradigm to work through the complexities related to the gender role discussion. I will not address that discussion in this study, except to use his examples to illustrate his method.

151 Ibid., 31.

152 Ibid., 65.

153 For a more developed and extended treatment of these potential issues, see Webb, *Slaves*.

154 We define essentials as those statements in our Statement of Faith that the elders have chosen to write down and document. If it is not documented, the topic is considered a non-essential.

155 Stackhouse, *Finally Feminist*, 24.

156 I recognize that these are glosses and the conversation is more complex. At the risk of being misunderstood, I present these as simple arguments to illustrate Stackhouse's proposal.

157 These are largely drawn from Stackhouse's work for purposes of illustration.

158 Turner, *Matthew*, 172.

159 Osborne, *Matthew*, 201.

160 Stackhouse, *Finally Feminist*, 36–38.

161 Ibid., 51. He resolves the dilemma by evaluating culture and backgrounds, although anyone familiar with the discussion knows that both sides have what they consider coherent and airtight biblical arguments.

162 Ibid., 34. Italics his.

163 Ibid. I have removed his parenthetical notes for simplicity.

164 Ibid., 72.

165 Stanley J. Grenz, *Renewing the Center: Evangelical Theology in a Post-Theological Era* (Grand Rapids, MI: Baker, 2000), 212. "Once formulated, however, the understanding of God as triune became a nonnegotiable dimension of church teaching."

166 For a comprehensive study on the historical position of the church, see S. Donald Fortson III and Rollin G. Grams, *Unchanging Witness: The Consistent Christian Teaching on Homosexuality in Scripture and Tradition* (Nashville, TN: B&H, 2016). Additionally, for a hermeneutical analysis on homosexuality throughout the Bible, see Webb, *Slaves*.

167 Stackhouse, *Finally Feminist*, 39.

Chapter 5

168 For example, see the following and many, many more. David Dark, *The Sacredness of Questioning Everything* (Grand Rapids, MI: Zondervan, 2009); Michael Dedivonai, *The Quest for Truth: Come Now and Let Us Reason Together* (Bloomington, IN: Authorhouse, 2005); John S. Feinberg, *Can You Believe It's True? Christian Apologetics in a Modern and Postmodern Era* (Wheaton, IL: Crossway, 2013); Douglas Groothuis, *Christian Apologetics: A Comprehensive Case for Biblical Faith* (Downers Grove, IL: InterVarsity, 2011); Michael Green, *But Don't All Religions Lead to God? Navigating the Multi-Faith Maze* (Grand Rapids, MI: Baker, 2002); Preston Jones, ed. *Is Belief in God Good, Bad or Irrelevant? A Professor and a Punk Rocker Discuss Science, Religion, Naturalism & Christianity* (Downers Grove, IL: InterVarsity, 2006); David Kinnaman and Aly Hawkins, *You Lost Me: Why Young Christians Are Leaving Church, and Rethinking Faith* (Grand Rapids, MI: Baker, 2011); David Kinnaman and Gabe Lyons, *Unchristian: What a New Generation Really Thinks About Christianity—and Why It Matters* (Grand Rapids, MI: Baker, 2007); Ravi K. Zacharias and Norman L. Geisler, *Is Your Church Ready? Motivating Leaders to Live an Apologetic Life* (Grand Rapids, MI: Zondervan, 2003).

169 Note, for example, Christopher Wright's work in missional theology and ethics. Wright, *Mission of God*; Christopher J. H. Wright, *The Mission of God's People: A Biblical Theology of the Church's Mission*, ed. Jonathan Lunde, Biblical Theology for Life (Grand Rapids, MI: Zondervan, 2010); Christopher J. H. Wright, *Knowing Jesus through the Old Testament*, 2d ed. (Downers Grove, IL: InterVarsity, 2014); Christopher J. H. Wright, *Old Testament Ethics for the People of God* (Downers Grove, IL: InterVarsity, 2004). Also, William Webb has done much work in the redemptive nature of God as expressed in Scripture. Webb, *Slaves*; William J. Webb, *Corporal Punishment in the Bible: A Redemptive-Movement Hermeneutic for Troubling Texts* (Downers Grove, IL: IVP Academic, 2011). N. T. Wright has become quite famous for his work on kingdom theology and how Christ has brought to reality what the Old Testament visualized all along.

170 This captures the helpful title of Grenz's work. Grenz, *Renewing*.

171 Ibid., 199.

172 Ibid., 202–03.

173 Ibid., 202.

174 Ibid., 203.

175 Ibid. Italics his.

176 Arland J. Hultgren, *Christ and His Benefits: Christology and Redemption in the New Testament* (Philadelphia, PA: Fortress, 1987), 193.

177 Grenz, *Renewing*, 216.

178 Ibid., 281.

179 Robert L. Hubbard Jr., "לאג," in *New International Dictionary of Old Testament Theology and Exegesis*, ed. Willem A. VanGemeren, (Grand Rapids, MI: Zondervan, 1996), vol. 1, 792.

180 "Λυτρόω," in *New International Dictionary of New Testament Theology and Exegesis*, ed. Moisés Silva, (Grand Rapids, MI: Zondervan, 2014), vol. 3, 185.

181 Richter, *Eden*, 89.

182 Philip Edgcumbe Hughes, *The True Image: The Origin and Destiny of Man in Christ* (Grand Rapids, MI and Leicester, England: Eerdmans and InterVarsity, 1989), 9.

183 Ibid., 391. Italics mine.

184 Ibid., 382.

185 Kilner, *Dignity*, 39.

186 Marc Cortez, *Theological Anthropology: A Guide for the Perplexed* (New York and London: T&T Clark, 2010), 17.

187 Kilner, *Dignity*, 40.

188 The traditional way of understanding this is with the language of accommodation. However, as I study Scripture, it seems that God goes beyond accommodation to actually compromising in what he ultimately desires.

189 Webb, *Slaves*.

190 Ibid., 22.

191 Webb used this example to illustrate how his redemptive-movement model works. Webb, *Corporal Punishment*, 79–80.

192 Jeffrey H. Tigay, *Deuteronomy: The Traditional Hebrew Text with the New JPS Translation*, ed. Nahum M. Sarna and Chaim Potok, The JPS Torah Commentary (Philadelphia, PA: Jewish Publication Society, 1996), 230.

193 Christopher J. H. Wright, *Deuteronomy*, ed. W. Ward Gasque, Robert L. Hubbard, Jr., and Robert K. Johnston, Understanding the Bible Commentary Series (Grand Rapids, MI: Baker, 1996), 264.

194 J. G. McConville, *Deuteronomy*, ed. David W. Baker and Gordon J. Wenham, Apollos Old Testament Commentary, vol. 5 (Leicester, England and Downers Grove, IL: Apollos and InterVarsity, 2002), 368.

195 Turner, *Matthew*, 167.

196 Craig Blomberg, *Matthew*, ed. David S. Dockery, New American Commentary (Nashville, TN: Broadman, 1992), 95.

197 Jewett and Kotansky, *Romans*, 58–59. See also C. E. B. Cranfield, *The Epistle to the Romans*, ed. J. A. Emerton and C. E. B. Cranfield, 2 vols., International Critical Commentary (Edinburgh: T. & T. Clark, 1975–79), 1:18–19; James D. G. Dunn, *Romans*, ed. David A. Hubbard, Glenn W. Barker, and Ralph P. Martin, 2 vols., Word Biblical Commentary (Dallas, TX: Word Books, 1988), 1:xlv.

198 Jewett and Kotansky, *Romans*, 765–67.

199 Webb, *Corporal Punishment*, 66.

Chapter 6

200 Scot McKnight, *A Community Called Atonement*, ed. Tony Jones, Living Theology (Nashville, TN: Abingdon, 2007), 9. Italics his.

201 Kevin J. Vanhoozer, *The Drama of Doctrine: A Canonical-Linguistic Approach to Christian Theology* (Louisville, KY: Westminster John Knox, 2005), xi.

202 Willem VanGemeren, *The Progress of Redemption: The Story of Salvation from Creation to the New Jerusalem* (Grand Rapids, MI: Baker, 1988), 357. Italics mine.

203 Wells, *No Place*, 218–57.

204 Vanhoozer, *Drama*, xiii. Italics his.

205 Ibid., 58.

206 In this section, I will follow parts of McKnight's very accessible and helpful work, *Kingdom Conspiracy*. Scot McKnight, *Kingdom Conspiracy: Returning to the Radical Mission of the Local Church* (Grand Rapid, MI: Brazos, 2014), 66.

207 Ibid., 75. McKnight credits Paul Minear's classic work which identified ninety-six different images of the church. Paul S. Minear, *Images of the Church in the New Testament* (Philadelphia, PA: Westminster, 1960).

208 Turner, *Matthew*, 429.

209 Osborne, *Matthew*, 664.

210 Ben Witherington, *Conflict and Community in Corinth: A Socio-Rhetorical Commentary on 1 and 2 Corinthians* (Grand Rapids, MI: Eerdmans, 1995), 24.

211 Ibid., 30.

212 Gordon D. Fee, *The First Epistle to the Corinthians*, ed. Joel B. Green, Rev. ed., New International Commentary on the New Testament (Grand Rapids, MI: Eerdmans, 2014), 158–59.

213 Witherington, *1 and 2 Corinthians*, 134.

214 Peter T. O'Brien, *The Letter to the Ephesians*, ed. D. A. Carson, Pillar New Testament Commentary (Grand Rapids and Leicester: Eerdmans and Apollos, 1999), 220.

215 Daniel I. Block, *Deuteronomy*, ed. Terry Muck, NIV Application Commentary (Grand Rapids, MI: Zondervan, 2012), 392.

216 Francis J. Moloney, *The Gospel of John*, ed. Daniel J. Harrington, Sacra Pagina (Collegeville, MN: Liturgical, 1998), 232–37.

217 Ibid., 235.

218 Ibid., 413. Italics mine.

219 N. T. Wright, *How God Became King: The Forgotten Story of the Gospels* (New York: HarperOne, 2012), 127.

220 McKnight, *Conspiracy*, 111.

221 Wolfhart Pannenberg, *Theology and the Kingdom of God* (Philadelphia, PA: Westminster, 1969), 72. Italics mine.

222 Ibid., 75.

223 I am grateful for my colleague, Don Payne, for his thinking in this area.

224 Grenz, *Renewing*, 278.

225 Ibid., 281.

226 Ibid., 282.

227 O'Brien, *Ephesians*, 170.

228 Wright, *Mission of God's People*, 129.

Chapter 7

229 Leslie C. Allen, *Jeremiah: A Commentary*, ed. William P. Brown, Carol A. Newsom, and David L. Peterson, Old Testament Library (Louisville, KY and London: Westminster John Knox, 2008), 322; J. Andrew Dearman, *Jeremiah and Lamentations*, ed. Terry Muck, The NIV Application Commentary (Grand Rapids, MI: Zondervan, 2002), 261; J. A. Thompson, *The Book of Jeremiah*, The New International Commentary on the Old Testament (Grand Rapids, MI: William B. Eerdmans, 1980; reprint, 1989), 544.

230 Dearman, *Jeremiah, Lamentations*, 262.

231 Thompson, *Jeremiah*, 546.

232 Allen, *Jeremiah*, 324.

233 Pannenberg, *Kingdom*, 102.

234 McKnight, *Conspiracy*, 111.

235 Ibid., 203.

236 Miroslav Volf, "Human Flourishing," in *Renewing the Evangelical Mission*, ed. Richard Lints, (Grand Rapids, MI: Eerdmans, 2013), 30. Italics his.

237 Vanhoozer, *Drama*, 394. Italics his.

238 Jürgen Moltmann, "Christianity: A Religion of Joy," in *Joy and Human Flourishing: Essays on Theology, Culture, and the Good Life*, ed. Miroslav Volf and Justin E. Crisp, (Minneapolis, MN: Fortress, 2015), 6.

239 Ibid., 11.

240 Marianne Meye Thompson, "Reflections on Joy in the Bible," in *Joy and Human Flourishing: Essays on Theology, Culture, and the Good Life*, ed. Miroslav Volf and Justin E. Crisp, (Minneapolis, MN: Fortress, 2015), 20.

241 Moltmann, "Human Flourishing," 14.

242 Ibid.

243 Miroslav Volf, "The Crown of the Good Life: A Hypothesis," in *Joy and Human Flourishing: Essays on Theology, Culture, and the Good Life*, ed. Miroslav Volf and Justin E. Crisp, (Minneapolis, MN: Fortress, 2015), 129.

244 Volf, "Flourishing," 30. Italics his.

245 Plantinga, *Not the Way*, 37.

246 Wright, *Mission of God's People*, 114–27.

247 Ibid., 128–47.

248 Moloney, *John*, 243. Italics mine.

249 Grenz, *Renewing*, 337.

Appendix 1

250 I had never considered these as possible examples of compromise until this conference. Therefore, I am indebted to these pastors who took the exercise seriously and we all grew as a result.

Scripture Index

Subject Index

CPSIA information can be obtained
at www.ICGtesting.com
Printed in the USA
BVHW070913080221
599618BV00015B/867